I0129231

Horace Piper

**Genealogy of Elisha Piper, of Parsonsfield, Me., and His Descendants**

Including portions of other related families, with an appendix, containing

genealogies of Asa Piper, of Wakefield, N. H., Solomon Piper, of Boston, Mass.,

Stephen Piper, of Newfie

Horace Piper

**Genealogy of Elisha Piper, of Parsonsfield, Me., and His Descendants**
*Including portions of other related families, with an appendix, containing genealogies of Asa Piper, of Wakefield, N. H., Solomon Piper, of Boston, Mass., Stephen Piper, of Newfie*

ISBN/EAN: 9783337317539

Printed in Europe, USA, Canada, Australia, Japan

Cover: Foto ©ninafisch / pixelio.de

More available books at **www.hansebooks.com**

# GENEALOGY

OF

# ELISHA PIPER,

## OF PARSONSFIELD, ME.,

### AND

# ☞ HIS DESCENDANTS, ☜

INCLUDING PORTIONS OF OTHER RELATED FAMILIES.

---

# WITH AN APPENDIX,

CONTAINING THE GENEALOGIES OF

ASA PIPER, OF WAKEFIELD, N. H.,
SOLOMON PIPER, OF BOSTON, MASS.,
STEPHEN PIPER, OF NEWFIELD, ME.,

### AND

THEIR IMMEDIATE DESCENDANTS.

---

FROM 1630 TO 1889.

---

BY HORACE PIPER, A. M.

———————

WASHINGTON, D. C.:
1889.

# CONTENTS.

(3)

# PREFACE.

I have had three principal objects in view in the preparation of this book :

1st. To make a complete and reliable genealogical record of Elisha¹ Piper and his descendants, with portions of other related families. To effect this object, much correspondence has been held, and many early records searched, at considerable expense. In the genealogies of our early ancestors, some dates could not be found, as the family records have been lost or have not been made, and when stones have been erected to their memories, only the date of their death and their age in years have generally been inscribed upon them, and therefore the exact time of their birth could not be ascertained, although it is as essential as the date of their death. This fact suggests the importance of giving the exact date of the birth and of the death. The age in years should also be stated, to save the person who reads the inscription the trouble of calculating it mentally. The surname of the wife before marriage, as well as the Christian name, should also be given, since it is often as important, in tracing families, to know the name of the wife as that of the husband. I have also had in view the importance of making a record which would be likely to be preserved. When genealogical records are made of individual families only, and recorded on a single sheet or in a single book, they are frequently lost, or destroyed by fire or other accident, in a few years, rendering it very difficult, and often impossible to replace them ; but if they have been collected and printed in a book, and many copies distributed among various persons, or deposited in libraries, it is not probable that they would all be lost for many years—perhaps for centuries.

2d. To give a history of the family. It is a moral and religious duty which we owe to our friends to become acquainted with those living, and to preserve in our memories the names of those who

have departed, that they may not be forgotten, or be lost to future generations by long lapse of time. With this view I have collected all the history of the family which I have been able to obtain, and given it principally in the remarks which I have made concerning the persons whose genealogies I have recorded. I cannot trace the family, with certainty, beyond Nathaniel Piper, our English ancestor in this country, whose genealogy and history are given on page 11. I have thought, however, that it might be interesting, and perhaps throw some light on our ancestral origin, if I should give some facts relating to the Pipers in England. The name of Piper is quite common in that country. Burke, in his "General Armory of England, Scotland, Ireland and Wales," mentions, in the last edition (1878), seven families of that name, residing in different counties, which have been permitted, by the Sovereign of Great Britain, to bear a coat of arms. The family with which we are especially interested resides in Devonshire, from which county Nathaniel Piper emigrated to this country. It is called the Culliton House, or family, from the town of Culliton in which the estate is located, being a few miles east of Exeter. The estate was purchased of Sir John De la Pole, baronet of Shute, by John Piper, Esq. The family traces its lineage from Magnus Piper, of Neustadt, in Holstein, formerly a part of Saxony, whose ancestors were from Lubeck. The coat of arms borne by the Culliton family is described by Burke as follows : " Quarterly, embattled gold and ermine, over all an eagle displayed sable, quartering azure, two chevrons gold." The motto is, *Feroci fortior*, or, More brave than fierce.

John Piper, Esq., was born in 1740, and was a Captain in the 6th Regiment of Infantry. He was destined at an early age for the military profession, and sent to Berlin where he completed a scientific and military course of study. In 1757 he entered the army, and fought in the battle of Minden in Prussia, where he was wounded through both legs. He afterward served in the West Indies, participating in the capture of Martinique. He also served in America, to which he came in the 25th Regiment, in 1769, and was appointed to the staff. While in this country, he married Frances Ayrault, second daughter and co-heiress of Stephen Ayrault, Esq., of Newport, Rhode Island, the only remaining representative of a distinguished and opulent Huguenot family. He returned from this country to England with his wife in 1782, and retired from

military life in 1788, to the Culliton estate, where he lived with his family till his death in 1802.

He had by his wife, Frances, three sons: 1st, John Piper, born in 1783. He was knighted with the title of C. B., and was Colonel of the 4th or King's Own Regiment of Infantry. He served in Canada, Holland, Denmark, Flanders, Spain, Portugal, France, and the West Indies; and finally fell a sacrifice to the pernicious effects of climate, in 1821, in the thirty-eighth year of his age, his death being hastened by exhaustion from the last and almost mortal wound which he received in the vertebræ of the neck, in the neighborhood of Bayonne, in Nov., 1813. 2d, Samuel Ayrault Piper, born in 1787. He was Surgeon of the 30th Regiment of his Majesty's troops. 3d, Robert Sloper Piper, born in 1790. He was Major of the Corps of Royal Engineers, and served in six campaigns under the Duke of Wellington, in Spain, France, and Flanders. He was also Commanding Engineer in the Canadian Province during the insurrection in 1817 and 1818. He retired on full pay, as Lieut. Colonel.*

I have not been able to ascertain whether Nathaniel' Piper is related to this family or not, but the fact that it resides in the same county from which he emigrated to this country, and that the names, John and Samuel, are found in both families, and have been retained as favorite names in a large number of the families of the descendants of Nathaniel' Piper, renders it possible that both families are descended from the same common ancestor, Magnus Piper of Holstein. There is no doubt, however, that both are of Saxon or Anglo-Saxon origin.

3d. To call the attention of the family to the importance of striving to elevate it to a higher degree of usefulness and distinction. It has doubtless accomplished as much as most families, but a higher degree of excellence is needed than it has yet attained. This must be accomplished principally by education. It is true that children generally inherit the intellectual qualities of their parents, and those children are fortunate whose parents possess superior minds; but the subject of heredity, although it is important and should not be overlooked. is not so fully under our control as that of ed-

* Most of the facts here related of the Culliton family have been taken from "Burke's General Armory," and his "Genealogical and Heraldic Dictionary of the Landed Gentry of Great Britain and Ireland."

ucation. The idea of the importance of a good education should be impressed on the minds of the young at an early age. It is one of the first duties of parents to educate their children. They should be ambitious to make them intelligent and useful. No parents should be satisfied with giving their children less education than would fit them to teach a common school, whatever occupation they are expected to pursue : and all should endeavor to give some of them the best which the institutions of their State or country afford. Their moral faculties, as well as their intellectual, should be developed by a thorough moral and religious training. They should feel that their duties as parents have not been fully discharged until they have done all this. It is believed by intellectual philosophers that mental development acquired by education is, in some degree, transmitted to the offspring; and, if this is so, as I have no doubt it is, there will be a constant intellectual growth of the family in succeeding generations to an extent that cannot now be known.

The record of the genealogy of Elisha[4] Piper and his descendants ends when neither of the parents of the children has the name of Piper, for in that case, having no immediate ancestors of that name, they would belong wholly to another family. I have, however, given the genealogy of a few children of this class in notes at the bottom of the pages, whose names were sent to me with the expectation that they would be included. In the Appendix I have given the genealogy of Asa[4] Piper, of Wakefield, N. H.: of Solomon[3] Piper, of Boston, Mass.; and of Stephen[3] Piper, of Newfield, Me., and their immediate descendants, but have extended them no farther, as to have done so would have required more time than I could possibly devote to them.

Much time and labor have been expended in collecting the genealogies of the various families, and had I not been assisted by others, it would have been almost impossible for me to have obtained all of them. While I am grateful to all who have assisted me, my thanks are especially due to William T.[6] Piper, of Cambridge, Mass., son of Solomon[3] Piper, of Boston, who has searched early records, and furnished me much information never before published, and also given me the use of his father's "Genealogy of the Family of Solomon[4] Piper, of Dublin, N. H.," from which I have copied freely; to Hiram H.[7] Piper, of Malden, Ill., who has furnished me the genealogies of a large number of the Pipers in that State ; to George F.[6]

Piper for the genealogy of the descendants of Asa[4] Piper, of Wakefield, N. H.; to Lewis L.[3] Piper for the genealogy of those of Stephen[5] Piper, of Newfield, Me.; to Noah P.[7] Young, of Stratham, N. H., who has searched the records of Stratham, visited neighboring towns for information, and furnished me the genealogies of several of the Piper families of that town; to Miss Harriet C. Brown, of Cincinnati, Ohio, for the history and genealogy of the Moffatt families and of the family of her father; and to Mrs. Mary Thaxter[5] (Jemegan) McGill for the genealogy and history of David[5] Piper, her grandfather, and of several other families of his descendants, besides her own family. All the genealogical records given in this book have been brought down from 1630 to the present time, 1889, embracing a period of more than two hundred and fifty years.

H. P.

Washington, D. C., Sept. 26, 1889.

# EXPLANATIONS.

The numbers on the left of the page are the serial numbers of the persons whose genealogies are given in the book ; those in Roman letters are the numbers of the children in each family ; those in parenthesis refer *back* to the same serial numbers on the left, where the genealogies of the parents are given ; those following, " See their children," refer *forward* to the same serial numbers on the left, where the genealogies of the children are given ; the small elevated figure at the right of the Christian name denotes the generation of the person from his English ancestor, Nathaniel[1] Piper, who is the first generation of the family in this country ; when nothing is said of the death of a person, the person is now ( 1889) living ; when nothing of the marriage, the person has not been married. This rule in regard to marriage has been observed, except in a few cases of our early ancestors, where it could not be known whether they were married or not, and in some few of the notes at the bottom of the pages.

# GENEALOGY OF ELISHA⁴ PIPER,

## AND HIS DESCENDANTS.

———

### FIRST GENERATION.

**1.** NATHANIEL¹ PIPER, ancestor of Elisha⁴ Piper, and so far as I have been able to ascertain, of nearly all the Pipers in this country. was born in England, probably about 1630. He emigrated from Dartmouth, in Devonshire, and settled in Ipswich, Mass., as a farmer. James Savage, in his Genealogical Dictionary, represents him as being here in 1665. Solomon² Piper, author of the Genealogy of the Family of Solomon⁴ Piper, says : " He drew a share and a half in Plum Island in 1665, and was an early inhabitant of Ipswich, Mass." Rev. Asa⁴ Piper, of Wakefield, N. H., in his genealogical record, says : " He emigrated from England to this country during the Revolution in the days of Charles the First," under Oliver Cromwell, which could not have been later than 1658. William T.⁶ Piper, in a recent search of the Ipswich records, now in the Essex County Registry of Deeds, finds, Book II. p. 251, a deed of marsh land on Jaffrey's Neck, Ipswich, from Andrew Hodges to Nathaniel¹ Piper, dated March 18, 1662. Also, in the Suffolk County Registry of Deeds, Book I. p. 330, a deed from Martyn Stebens, of Boston, Mass., to Wm. Bartholomew, of Ipswich, dated Dec. 15, 1653, and witnessed by Nathaniel¹ Piper, which seems to prove conclusively that he came to this country as early as Dec. 15, 1653. He married Sarah* ——, and died in 1676, in Ipswich. His will, a copy of which is given in this book, and recorded in the Ipswich records, is dated March 7, 1675, and was proved, Sept. 26, 1676. After his decease his wife married Ezekiel Woodward, of Wenham, Mass., a carpenter. She was living in Wenham in 1696, and probably died there, but no record of the time of her death can be found. Her second husband, Ezekiel Woodward, died Jan. 29, 1698, in Wenham.—SEE THEIR CHILDREN : Nos. **2. 3. 4. 5. 6. 7. 8. 9. 10, 11, 12.**

* It is probable that he married his wife in this country, where all his children were born.

## SECOND GENERATION.

(**1.**) Nathaniel[1] Piper married Sarah ——.

THEIR CHILDREN :

**2.** i. SARAH[2] PIPER (*Nathaniel[1]*), born about 1656 in Ipswich, Mass.; was living in 1675, being under twenty-one years of age ; died.

**3.** ii. NATHANIEL[2] PIPER (*Nathaniel[1]*), born June 25, 1658, in Ipswich ; died probably about 1689, in Ipswich.  The children, with the consent of their mother Sarah, sold the homestead of their father to John Wainright, of Ipswich, the deed being dated June 18, 1690, and signed by John[2] Piper, Thomas[2] Piper, Mary[2] Piper, and Tristram Greenleaf, who married Margaret[2] Piper.  Nathaniel[2] Piper does not appear as a signer of the deed, nor does his name appear in it, although his father had given him by will a part of his property.  It would seem, therefore, that he had died before the farm was sold.  Rev. Asa[4] Piper speaks of three sons of Nathaniel[1] Piper, namely, Nathaniel[2], Thomas[2], and Samuel[2].  He says : "Two of them went to Stratham, N. H., and the other I believe died young." Nathaniel[2] may be the one who died young, that is, a young man.

**4.** iii. MARY[2] PIPER (*Nathaniel[1]*), born Nov. 5, 1660, in Ipswich ; died Feb. 18, 1661, in Ipswich.

**5.** iv. JOSIAH[2] PIPER (*Nathaniel[1]*), born Dec. 18, 1661, in Ipswich ; was living in 1675 ; died.

**6.** v. JOHN[2] PIPER* (*Nathaniel[1]*) born in 1663 in Ipswich ; married Lydia —— ; died probably in Wenham, Mass.  She died probably in Wenham.

**7.** vi. MARY[2] PIPER (*Nathaniel[1]*), born Dec. 15, 1664, in Ipswich ; was living in 1690 ; died.

**8.** vii. THOMAS[2] PIPER† (*Nathaniel[1]*), born Nov. 26, 1666, in Ipswich ; married Grace Hawley, of Wenham, Nov. 21, 1692 ; died perhaps in Stratham, N. H., and his wife in the same place.  It is

---

* John[2] has the name of one child recorded in the Wenham records : Sarah[3], born about 1686 in Wenham, Mass.; died June 5, 1695, in Wenham.

† Thomas[2] Piper has the names of three children recorded in the Wenham records :  1. Thomas[3], born Nov. 17, 1697, in Wenham, Mass.; died in Stratham, N. H.  2. Nathaniel[3], born Jan. 22, 1701, in Wenham ; died in Stratham.  3. Patience[3], born Feb. 25, 1703, in Ipswich, Mass.; died.  For additional particulars, see "Genealogy of Stephen[3] Piper, of Newfield", and his Immediate Descendants," Nos. 13, 14, 15.

not certainly known whether he went to Stratham or not; his son Thomas³ went there.

**9.** viii. MARGARET² PIPER ( *Nathaniel¹*), born June 16, 1668, in Ipswich; married Tristram Greenleaf Nov. 12, 1689; died; he died.

**10.** ix. SAMUEL² PIPER ( *Nathaniel¹*), grandfather of Elisha⁴ Piper, born June 12, 1670, in Ipswich; married Abigail Church,* April 23, 1694; died Oct. 31, 1747, in Stratham, N. H., to which place he removed probably a short time before the incorporation of the town. She died in Stratham. He last appears on the town records of Stratham, as a voter, in 1746. He was one of the signers of a petition, in 1715, to incorporate the town of Stratham, which was incorporated in 1716. He held several offices in town, as sealer of leather, surveyor of highways, and constable.—SEE THEIR CHILDREN: Nos. **13, 14, 15, 16.**

**11.** x. JONATHAN² PIPER† ( *Nathaniel¹*), born in Ipswich, probably in 1672; a farmer; married, 1st, Sarah Leach, of Boxford, Mass., May 7, 1695. She died May 6, 1700, in Ipswich. 2d, Alice Darbey, of Beverly, Mass., published Sept. 21, 1700; certificate granted Oct. 9, 1700. He died May 11, 1752, in Concord, Mass., to which place he removed from Ipswich in 1731. She died April 23, 1758, in Concord.

**12.** xi. WILLIAM² PIPER‡ ( *Nathaniel¹*), born in Ipswich; died Jan. 18, 1674, in Ipswich.

## THIRD GENERATION.

( **10.** ) Samuel² Piper married Abigail Church.

### THEIR CHILDREN:

**13.** i. SAMUEL³ PIPER ( *Samuel²*, *Nathaniel¹*), father of Elisha⁴ Piper, born according to the latest information obtained, probably in Ipswich, Mass., in 1701. He was baptized in Wenham in 1701, but some families living in the part of Ipswich near Wenham

---

* See Proceedings of Massachusetts Historical Society, Vol. XIV, p. 151.

† Jonathan² had nine children: 1. Samuel³; 2. Jonathan³; 3. Nathaniel³; 4. Josiah³; 5. John³; 6. Alice³; 7. Sarah³; 8. Mary³; 9. Joseph³. Joseph³ was grandfather of Solomon⁵ Piper, late of Boston, Mass. See "Genealogy of Solomon⁵ Piper, of Boston, Mass., and his Immediate Descendants," Nos. 13, 14, 15, 16, 17, 18, 19, 20, 21.

‡ William² and the first Mary² died before their father Nathaniel¹ made his will, and are therefore not mentioned in it. As the time of William's² birth is not known, I have placed his name last.

attended church in the latter place, as it was nearer than the church in Ipswich. He married Jane Cate, and lived in Stratham, N. H., as a farmer the most of his life, or till 1785, when he removed with his youngest son Samuel[4] to Loudon, N. H. He held some town offices in Stratham, as surveyor of highways, constable, &c. He died in Loudon about 1788. No record of the exact date of his death can be found. The one given does not vary much from the true one. His wife died in Stratham. The record of his baptism is found in the Wenham records.—SEE THEIR CHILDREN: Nos. 17, 18, 19, 20.

**14.** ii. JOHN[3] PIPER* (Samuel[2], Nathaniel[1]), born about 1703, [. . . .] Ipswich; married Jane Haines, daughter of Samuel Haines, of Greenland, N. H., Dec., 1729. She died March 20, 1741, in Stratham, N. H. He died Nov. 4, 1742, in Stratham, being drowned in the Great Bay.

**15.** iii. ABIGAIL[3] PIPER (Samuel[2], Nathaniel[1]), born about 1705, probably in Ipswich; died.

---

* John[3] Piper has the names of three children recorded : 1. John[4], baptized in 1736, in Greenland, N. H.; married, had a family, and died in Stratham, N. H. 2. Samuel[4], born June 21, 1739, in Stratham, died about 1829, in Stratham. 3. An infant child[4], born in Stratham : died March 16, 1741, in Stratham. The statement concerning John[3] Piper and his wife, and first and third child may be found in the "New England Historical and Genealogical Register," Vol. XXII, p. 431; concerning the second, in the Stratham records.

Richard Upton[6] Piper, M. D., is a descendant of John[3] Piper, as follows : Richard Upton[6], born April 3, 1818, in Stratham, N. H. Samuel[5], born Feb. 22, 1785, in Stratham : died about 1860, in Exeter, N. H. Samuel[4], born June 21, 1739, in Stratham ; died about 1829, in Stratham. John[3], born and died as stated above in No. 14. Samuel[2], born June 12, 1679, in Ipswich, Mass.; died Oct. 31, 1747, in Stratham. Nathaniel[1], born about 1630, in England ; died in 1676, in Ipswich. He graduated from the Medical Department of Dartmouth College in 1840 ; married Elizabeth Frances Folsom, daughter of Nathan Boardman and Sarah (Quincy) Folsom, Nov. 9, 1843. born March 7, 1819, in Portsmouth, N. H. He practiced medicine in Woburn, Mass. several years, and also in Chicago, Ill. He is an author, and published, in 1852, "Operative Surgery," 8vo., 378 pages, illustrated with about two thousand engravings, made by himself : in 1855, an edition of "Maclise's Surgical Anatomy," 4to., illustrated with plates of his own engraving ; in 1857, "The Trees of America," with illustrations ; and has also contributed articles to the "New Orleans Medical Journal" and other scientific publications. He has given much attention to the study of microscopy, and is an expert in that science, being often called to make microscopic examinations in cases in courts

**16.** iv. SARAH³ PIPER* (*Samuel²*, *Nathaniel¹*,) born about 1707, probably in Ipswich ; married Capt. Thomas Wiggin.  Both probably died in Stratham.

## FOURTH GENERATION.

(**13.**) Samuel³ Piper married Jane Cate.

THEIR CHILDREN :

**17.** i. JONATHAN⁴ PIPER (*Samuel³*, *Samuel²*, *Nathaniel¹*,) born July 31, 1742, in Stratham N. H. ; a farmer ; married Olive Light, of Exeter, N. H., born April 12, 1752 ; died in Stratham.  She died in Stratham.—SEE THEIR CHILDREN : Nos. **21, 22, 23, 24, 25, 26, 27, 28, 29, 30, 31, 32, 33, 34.**

**18.** ii. SAMUEL⁴ PIPER (*Samuel³*, *Samuel²*, *Nathaniel¹*), born Sept. 24, 1753, in Stratham ; married Sally Norris Feb. 15, 1781,

of justice and elsewhere, on which he has made many reports.  He has several thousand drawings of various objects, made under the microscope and admirably executed, which have not yet been bound in book form, and issued to the public.  A writer in the " North American Review," in a notice of his works, says : "He has the eye of an artist, the hand of a draftsman, and the spirit of an enthusiast."  He resides in Washington, D. C  Stephen Howard⁵ Piper, a successful merchant of Exeter, N. H., born August, 1814, in Stratham, is a descendant of the same ancestors as Richard Upton⁶, being his brother.

Samuel⁵ Piper, before mentioned, grandfather of Richard Upton⁵, is a first cousin of Elisha⁴ Piper, of Parsonsfield, Me. (See p. 16, No. 26).  He married Mary Robinson, June, 1762, born Aug. 1, 1744 ; she died in Stratham.  His children, as recorded in the Stratham records, are : 1. Mary⁵, born May 19, 1763 : died April 16, 1766.  2. Jane⁵, born April 9, 1765.  3. John⁵, born July 16, 1767.  4. Mehitable⁵, born Nov. 15, 1769.  5. Mary⁵, born Feb. 23, 1772 : died Sept. 29, 1774.  6. Noah Robinson⁵, born Feb. 2, 1777 : died Sept. 16, 1778.  7. Nancy⁵, born May 3, 1779.  8. Sally⁵, born Aug. 6, 1782 ; died Nov. 14, 1782.  9. Samuel⁵, born Feb. 22, 1785.  10. Sally⁵, born Jan. 25, 1786.  All were born in Stratham.  None are living.

Samuel⁵ Piper, father of Richard Upton⁶, married Mary Folsom, and resided in Stratham most of his life, but removed to Exeter a few years before his death.  His wife died in Exeter several years after his decease.  His children are : 1. Stephen Howard⁶.  2. Richard Upton⁶.  3. Samuel Folsom⁶  4. A son⁶, died in infancy.  5. Simeon Francis⁶.  6. Mary Boardman⁶.  7. Hannah Robinson⁶.  8. Sarah Folsom⁶.  9. Victoria Anna⁶.  10. Caroline Elizabeth⁶.  All were born in Stratham.  There are now living, Stephen Howard⁶, Richard Upton⁶, Samuel Folsom⁶, Simeon Francis⁶, and Victoria Anna⁶.

* They had one child at least, named Abigail Church Wiggin⁴, born Aug. 28, 1737, and married Stephen⁴ Piper, June 20, 1754.—See " Genealogy of Stephen³ Piper, of Newfield, Me., and his Immediate Descendants." No. 16.

born May 28, 1756, in Stratham. Soon after his marriage he sold
the homestead farm in Stratham, and removed with his father to
Loudon, N. H. He was there a hotel keeper, town clerk, and se-
lectman eight years, from 1787 to 1794. He died about 1813, in
Loudon. She died May 3. 1843. in Loudon.—SEE THEIR CHIL-
DREN: Nos. **35. 36. 37. 38. 39. 40. 41. 42. 43.**

**19.** iii. COMFORT⁴ PIPER* (*Samuel³, Samuel², Nathaniel¹*), born
July 10, 1756, in Stratham N. H. ; married Joseph Norris in 1774.
born Jan. 31, 1753. in Stratham ; died in Stratham. He died in
the same place.—SEE THEIR CHILDREN : Nos. **44. 45. 46. 47.
48. 49. 50. 51. 52.**

**20.** iv. ELISHA⁴ PIPER† (*Samuel³, Samuel², Nathaniel¹,*) born
June 17, 1746, in Stratham ; married, 1st, Sarah Barker, daughter
of Ebenezer Barker‡, of Stratham. born in 1748. in Stratham ; died
Nov. 13, 1798, in Parsonsfield, Me., aged 50 years ; 2d, Olive Dyer,

* There were six other daughters, but I have not been able to learn the
order of their ages, nor anything about their genealogies. and little of
their history. Abigail⁴ married ——— Robinson ; Rachel⁴ is supposed
to have married Jeremiah Avery, who once lived in Parsonsfield, Me., in
the south-west part of the town, on lot No. 41 ; Jane⁴ married —— ——
Pottle ; one, name unknown, married ——— Merrill ; Betsey⁴ never
married. I do not know the name of the other, nor whom she married.

† Elisha⁴ Piper, in the order of age, would follow next after Jonathan⁴,
but in order to bring all his descendants together, I have introduced him
here.

‡ Ebenezer Barker lived and died in Stratham.— HIS CHILDREN :
1. Nathaniel, born in Stratham, N. H. ; settled in Enfield, N. H.
2. Noah, born in Stratham ; settled in Cornish, Me., in 1784.—CHIL-
DREN: 1. Noah, married Sally Clark. 2. Thomas, married Sally Ayer.
3. Enoch, married Sally Jewett, and was a member of Massachusetts
Legislature before Maine was separated from that State. 4. Humphrey,
married Sally Hodgdon. All are dead.

3. Ebenezer, born Aug. 21, 1758, in Stratham ; married widow Hannah
Brasbree (maiden name, Burleigh) ; settled in Cornish, in 1784.—CHIL-
DREN; 1. Betsey, born May 4. 1782 ; married Stephen Jewett ; removed to
Sidney, Me., died April 10, 1862. 2. Ezra, born Mar. 13. 1784 ; died Oct.
15, 1807. 3. Sarah, born Sept. 26, 1786 ; married Mark Pease as his second wife ; died in Sidney, Oct. 9, 1826. 4. Mary Johnson, born July 13,
1788 ; died Aug. 27, 1815. 5. William, born May 29, 1790 ; died Jan. 31,
1815. 6. Ebenezer, born May 23, 1792 ; married Hannah Jewett ; died
Aug. 15, 1865. 7. Nancy Clark, born Oct. 1, 1794 ; married Mark Pease
as his first wife ; died Jan. 29, 1822. 8. Olive, born Sept. 5, 1797 ; died
Dec. 30, 1855. 9. Cyrus Snell, born May 26, 1800 ; married Nancy Thurston Smith. He furnished me this genealogical record of the Barker

daughter of Thomas and Elizabeth (Melcher) Dyer,* of Biddeford, Me., born in 1758, in Biddeford ; died April 20, 1808, in Parsonsfield, aged 50.years; 3d, Rosannah Dyer, daughter of Thomas and Elizabeth (Melcher) Dyer, of Biddeford, Oct. 1, 1808, born July 15, 1767, in Biddeford ; died April 23, 1839, in Parsonsfield.

After he married his first wife he lived about five years in Stratham, and then purchased a farm in Wakefield, N. H., located not far from Province Pond. He removed there in the spring of 1772, and remained nearly nine years. The farm proving frosty and his prospects for supporting his family on such land being very discouraging, he resolved to sell, and find a home in a more favorable locality. He directed his course to Parsonsfield, then called Parsonstown, in the province of Maine, at that time belonging to Massachusetts.

family about two years before his death, which occurred Aug. 21, 1880, at the age of 89 years. He was a man of high integrity and much respected. All are dead.

4. Simeon, born in 1768, in Stratham ; married Hannah Rundlet ; settled in Cornish. Me., in 1784, but subsequently removed to Limerick. Me., and died there in 1812.—CHILDREN : 1. Mary, married Daniel Perry. 2. Simeon, born Nov. 14, 1792 ; deacon of the Congregational Church in Limerick and Senator in the Maine Legislature ; married Almira Boardman, of Newburyport. Mass., born Oct. 1, 1800 ; died Mar. 19, 1884. He died July 15, 1856, in Limerick, where he resided. 3. Hannah, married Warwick Hobbs, of Wells. Me. 4. Sarah, never married. 5. Betsey, married John Jewett. 6. Susan, born May 21, 1802 ; married George Washington Drake, of Effingham, N. H. She is now living (1889) in Portsmouth, N. H. 7. Levi, married Olive Storer. He died in Arlington, Mass. 8. Charles, born in Limerick ; was twice married ; died in Fairfield, Me. All, except Susan, are dead.

5. Sarah, married Elisha⁴ Piper, as before stated.—SEE THEIR CHILDREN : Nos. 53, 54, 55, 56, 57, 58, 59, 60, 61, 62.

6 A daughter, born in Stratham ; married ―――― Wiggin, of Stratham. They died.

7. A daughter, born in Stratham ; married ―――― Berry, of Meredith, N. H. They died.

8. Hannah, born in Stratham ; married Thomas Ayers Johnson, of Cornish, Me.—CHILDREN : 1. Sarah, married Capt. James Wedgwood, of Parsonsfield, Me. 2. Olive, married Jonathan Garland, of Winslow, Me. 3. William, married Nancy Pike. 4. Augustus, married Mary Hodgdon. He was a member of the Maine Legislature. All, I think, are dead.

The sons of the first Ebenezer Barker are arranged in the order of their ages, and the daughters next in the order of theirs, although some of the daughters are older than some of the sons. He had other children, but their names not being known, they have been omitted.

* Thomas Dyer, who was published to Elizabeth Melcher Nov. 28, 1741.

He first purchased lot No. 25, in the second range, of Benjamin Hilton, of Parsonsfield, for one hundred and twenty-five pounds,* the deed being dated Nov. 5, 1778, and on this lot he settled. He subsequently purchased five other lots,—lot No. 171, in the tenth range, of Alpheus Spring, of Kittery, Me., for five pounds, deed dated Nov. 28, 1785; lot No. 51, in the third range, of John Brown, of Parsonsfield, for five hundred dollars, deed dated May 13, 1790 ; lot No. 13, in the first range, which was a tax sale, for six shillings and two pence, deed dated June 27, 1791 ; lot No. 88, in the fifth range, of Chase Wiggin, of Stratham, N. H., for forty-five pounds, deed dated Feb. 15, 1793; lot No. 50, in third range, which I do not find recorded in the County Registry of Deeds, although it is probably there. It now forms a large part of the old homestead.

In June 1779, the next year after his first purchase, he went from Wakefield to Parsonsfield, built him a log camp, covered with hemlock bark, felled several acres of trees, and then returned to his family in Wakefield. In March of the next year, 1780, he went back to Parsonsfield. As there were no roads passable for teams at that season of the year, he hauled his camp furniture, consisting of a bed and some cooking utensils, on a hand-sled, over Ricker's Mountain, on the crust. This was a great hardship, and he was obliged to get some assistance in his passage over the mountain. Before the time arrived for burning the trees, felled the preceding season, he was employed in preparing materials for building a log-house for his family. He burned the trees in May, and planted the ground with

lived in Biddeford, Me., at Winter Harbor, on the Pool Road, left hand side when going down, between two and two and a half miles from the Pool, by the road, and about a mile in a straight line. The house is still standing, and is owned by Joseph Edwards. All the vessels going out of Saco River can be seen from the door. He had quite a family. Besides Olive and Rosannah, there were Elizabeth, published to Caleb Locke, of Hollis, Me., Jan. 1, 1762 ; Miriam, to William Wadlin, of Biddeford, Feb. 20, 1770 ; Mary, to Phineas Downs, of Hollis, Dec. 4, 1771 ; Sarah, to Jeremiah Gilpatrick, of Limerick, Me., in 1775 ; Abigail, to ——— Coburn, of Kennebunk, Me., time unknown ; Thomas, an only son, who married, and died by drowning in Saco River, leaving two sons, Thomas and Oliver, and one daughter, Abigail. Capt. Ira C. Doe, of Saco, married a daughter of Thomas, last named. All those mentioned, except the last two, I think are dead. These facts, copied from the Biddeford records, have been kindly furnished me by Stephen Locke, of Biddeford, grandson of Caleb Locke who married Elizabeth Dyer.

* The value of a pound at that time was about three dollars, thirty-three and one third cents.

corn and such other crops as would be needed for the support of his family the next winter. His planting was all completed before the nineteenth of May, which was the famous Dark Day* of 1780, of which I have heard him speak with much earnestness, as being a very wonderful phenomenon. On that day he was helping his neighbor, George Bickford, finish planting his corn. After his crops had been harvested and his log-house completed, he returned to Wakefield to remove his family, consisting of his wife and six small children. He moved with an ox-team on the snow, late in the year 1780—probably in December, as the day is represented as having been bitter cold—the coldest of that winter. The suffering of the little children must have been severe, but such exposures often occur in pioneer life.

He had now settled down in a permanent home, and was about to enter upon a career of prosperity unknown to him before. He was thirty-two years of age when he purchased his farm in 1778, and his wife about two years younger, both being full of energy and hope, and ambitious of success. Farming was a business in which he delighted, and he pursued it successfully and scientifically, although he had never received any instruction in scientific farming. His land was fertile, and free from frost ; and his crops were abundant. The log-house was succeeded, in a few years, by a neat one-story frame-house, and finally about 1817 a story was added to this, and the whole neatly finished and painted. It is still standing, and is occupied by his great-grandson, Samuel Fullerton⁷ Piper. The lower story is nearly or quite a hundred years old.

To each of two of his sons he gave a farm, and assisted the others in purchasing farms for themselves. To each of his daughters he gave the usual sum, at that time, of one hundred dollars, as her marriage portion. He always kept money by him, usually not less than one hundred dollars ; and sometimes I have known him to have five hundred, derived from the sale of stock and farm products. He did

---

*The darkness began about ten o'clock in the forenoon, and continued about fourteen hours. It was so great that candles had to be lighted, common print could not be read, fowls retired to their roost, and cattle returned to the barn. Its cause has never been satisfactorily explained. It was not an eclipse. Meteorologists think it was caused by a very dense vapor, charged perhaps with foreign matter. The theory that smoke, in connection with vapor, was the cause has been more favorably received than any other. See an interesting account of it in a work entitled. "Our First Century."

not permit any of his neighbors to be in advance of him in his farm work, or surpass him in their farm products.   His farm stock was of the best breeds, and carefully selected ; and having a good pasturage, and being fed in winter on hay of the best quality, it was unsurpassed, in size and beauty, by any in the town.   It therefore sold for the highest market prices.   He kept one hired man through the year, and in the haying season, one additional, and sometimes two, if needed to secure the crop at the best time for cutting it ; so that his haying was generally finished by the end of July or the first week in August ; and his hay was of the choicest kind.   In 1796 he paid the largest tax of any man in the town, and was always among the largest tax-payers.

His first wife was a large woman, with dark hair and black eyes. She was the mother of ten children, five sons and five daughters, all of whom lived to be married, and have families ; and three of them lived to be over eighty years of age.   His other two wives were also large women, and all of them managed their household affairs with economy and ability.   In person he was of medium size, quick and active, and of the pure Anglo-Saxon type.   He was prompt in all his business transactions and private duties, and never omitted to ask a blessing at the table.   To the needy he was kind and benevolent, and none ever went away from his house hungry.   He died of old age March 10, 1836, in Parsonsfield where he had always lived after leaving Wakefield, N. H.—SEE THEIR CHILDREN : Nos. **53, 54, 55, 56, 57, 58, 59, 60, 61, 62.**

## FIFTH GENERATION.

(**17.**) Jonathan⁴ Piper married Olive Light.

THEIR CHILDREN :

**21.** i. JOHN LIGHT⁵ PIPER (*Jonathan⁴, Samuel³, Samuel², Nathaniel¹*), born March 23, 1771, in Stratham, N. H. ; died.

**22.** ii. DEBORAH⁵ PIPER (*Jonathan⁴, Samuel³, Samuel², Nathaniel¹*), born Feb. 7, 1773, in Stratham ; died.

**23.** iii. OLIVE⁵ PIPER (*Jonathan⁴, Samuel³, Samuel², Nathaniel¹*), born March 10, 1775, in Stratham ; died.

**24.** iv. JANE⁵ PIPER (*Jonathan⁴, Samuel³, Samuel², Nathaniel¹*), born Feb. 1, 1777, in Stratham ; died.

**25.** v. SAMUEL⁵ PIPER (*Jonathan⁴, Samuel³, Samuel², Nathaniel¹*), born March 8, 1779, in Stratham ; died.

**26.** vi. JONATHAN⁵ PIPER *(Jonathan⁴, Samuel³, Samuel², Nathaniel¹)*, born Jan. 21, 1781, in Stratham ; died.

**27.** vii. NOAH⁵ PIPER* *(Jonathan⁴, Samuel³, Samuel², Nathaniel¹)*, born Sept. 13, 1782, in Stratham ; a farmer and Christian Baptist minister. He was ordained in 1812, and was pastor of the Christian Baptist Church in Stratham, for about forty years. He also represented the town of Stratham in the State Legislature three years, and was several years county treasurer. He was deeply interested in his ministerial work, and emphatically a good man. In person he was tall, but spare. He married, 1st, Mary Crimbell, April 12, 1820, born July 19, 1791, in North Hampton, N. H.; died Aug. 12, 1836, in Stratham ; 2d. Hannah Crimbell, April 18, 1837, born April 23, 1786, in North Hampton ; died April 30, 1863, in Stratham. He died March 25, 1865, in Stratham, where he resided.

**28.** viii. SALLY⁵ PIPER *(Jonathan⁴, Samuel³, Samuel², Nathaniel¹)* born Sept. 2, 1784, in Stratham ; died.

**29.** ix. ABIGAIL⁵ PIPER *(Jonathan⁴, Samuel³, Samuel², Nathaniel¹)*, born March 5, 1786, in Stratham ; died.

**30.** x. BETSEY⁵ PIPER *(Jonathan⁴, Samuel³, Samuel², Nathaniel¹)*, born Jan. 15, 1788, in Stratham ; died.

**31.** xi. JOANNA⁵ PIPER *(Jonathan⁴, Samuel³, Samuel², Nathaniel¹)*, born Jan. 13, 1790, in Stratham ; died.

*NOAH⁵ PIPER'S CHILDREN :

1. Olive Light⁶, born Aug. 5, 1822, in Stratham, N. H. ; married Mark Furnald Young, Sept. 7, 1845, born March 21, 1817, in Tuftonborough, N. H. ; a farmer. He died April 10, 1876. She died Feb. 2, 1886. Both died in Stratham, where they resided.—THEIR CHILDREN : 1. John Edwin⁷, born Aug. 28, 1846, in Tuftonborough ; died July 29, 1851, in Tuftonborough. 2. Hannah Augusta⁷, born Dec. 9, 1848, in Tuftonborough; married Mark G. Roberts Nov. 28, 1872, born Dec. 15, 1839, in Stratham ; a farmer. He resides in Stratham. 3. Mary Crimbell⁷, born Nov. 7, 1850, in Tuftonborough ; resides in Stratham. 4. Noah Piper⁷, born July 28, 1853, in Stratham ; a farmer. He has rendered me valuable assistance in collecting genealogies for this book. See p. 9. He resides in Stratham. 5. John Edwin⁷, born Jan. 26, 1855, in Stratham. He resides in Exeter, Florida. 6. Olive Jane⁷, born Dec. 4, 1860, in Stratham ; married James Clark Piper Jan. 5, 1881, born Dec. 7, 1865, in Oskaloosa, Iowa ; a farmer. He resides in Stratham. 7. Sarah Lizzie⁷, born Feb. 7, 1863, in Stratham, and resides there.

2. Hannah Dearborn⁶, born April 14, 1829, in Stratham ; married Stephen W. Nudd, Sept. 9, 1846 ; died in Boston, Mass. She died June 24, 1847, in Boston, where they resided. They had one child.

**32.** xii. POLLY[5] PIPER (*Jonathan*[4], *Samuel*[3], *Samuel*[2], *Nathaniel*[1]), born May 16, 1792, in Stratham; died.

**33.** xiii. MARK WALTON[5] PIPER (*Jonathan*[4], *Samuel*[3], *Samuel*[2], *Nathaniel*[1]), born March 18, 1794, in Stratham; died.

**34.** xiv. EBENEZER SMITH[5] PIPER (*Jonathan*[4], *Samuel*[3], *Samuel*[2], *Nathaniel*[1]) born May 6, 1796, in Stratham; died.

(**18.**) Samuel[4] Piper married Sally Norris.

THEIR CHILDREN:

**35.** i. JONATHAN[5] PIPER (*Samuel*[4], *Samuel*[3], *Samuel*[2], *Nathaniel*[1]), born May 22, 1784, in Stratham, N. H. : died in March, 1861.

**36.** ii. BENJAMIN[5] PIPER (*Samuel*[4], *Samuel*[3], *Samuel*[2], *Nathaniel*[1]), born April 1, 1786, in Loudon, N. H. ; died.

**37.** iii. SALLY[5] PIPER (*Samuel*[4], *Samuel*[3], *Samuel*[2], *Nathaniel*[1]), born March 9, 1788, in Loudon; married Anthony Sherman Feb. 3, 1808 ; died ; he died.

**38.** iv. JANE[5] PIPER (*Samuel*[4], *Samuel*[3], *Samuel*[2], *Nathaniel*[1]), born Sept. 21, 1789, in Loudon; married Nathaniel Sherburne Mor. 4, 1813 : died ; he died.

**39.** v. BETSEY[5] PIPER (*Samuel*[4], *Samuel*[3], *Samuel*[2], *Nathaniel*[1]),

3. Jonathan[5], born Oct. 7, 1830, in Stratham ; married Sophia Antoinette Clark, Feb. 27, 1856, born May 26, 1838, in Giles County, Tenn ; a teacher before marriage. He was formerly a teacher, but is now connected with Ivison, Blakeman & Co., of Chicago, in the book business. He resides in Chicago, Ill.—THEIR CHILDREN : 1. Mary Jane[7], born July 23, 1857, in St. Francisville, Mo.; a teacher. 2. Lizzie Avery[7], born Sept. 19, 1859, in St. Francisville ; a teacher. 3. Nettie Clark[7], born May 1, 1862, in Eddyville, Iowa ; died Dec. 1, 1867, in Eddyville. 4. Noah[7], born May 22, 1864, in Eddyville ; married Olive Jeannette Byrnes, Feb. 17, 1887, born May 5, 1866, in Manitowoc, Wis. He is engaged in railroad business. 5. James Clark[7], born Dec. 7, 1866, in Oskaloosa, Iowa ; a farmer ; married Olive Jane[7] Young, Jan. 5, 1884, born Dec. 4, 1860, in Stratham, where they reside. 6. Harriet Rebecca[7], born Nov. 20, 1867, in Manchester, Iowa. 7. Jonathan Lane[7], born Nov. 26, 1868, in Manchester. 8. Olive Elfrida[7], born Dec. 7, 1876, in Wheaton, Ill. All except James Clark[7] reside in Chicago.

(4. NOAH[7] PIPER'S CHILD : Jonathan[8], born Jan. 8, 1888, in Belvidere, Ill.)

(5. JAMES CLARK[7] PIPER'S CHILDREN : 1. Mark Furnald[8], born Aug. 5, 1884. 2. Jonathan[8], born Aug. 11, 1885. 3. James Edwin[8], born Oct. 26, 1886. All were born in Oskaloosa, Iowa.)

4. Mary Jane[6], born Dec. 28, 1832, in Stratham ; died Jan. 1, 1874, in Northwood, N. H. She was never married.

born March 8, 1791, in Loudon ; married Lewis Flanders Feb. 6, 1812. She died March 31, 1877, in Readfield, Me. ; he died.

**40.** vi. SAMUEL[5] PIPER* (*Samuel[4]*, *Samuel[3]*, *Samuel[2]*, *Nathaniel[1]*), born March 22, 1792, in Loudon ; married Martha W. Brown, born March 6, 1802, in Pittsfield, N. H. He died Jan. 29, 1874. She died in Loudon, N. H. in 1888.

**41.** vii. DAVID NORRIS[5] PIPER† (*Samuel[4]*, *Samuel[3]*, *Samuel[2]*, *Nathaniel[1]*), born Aug. 26, 1794 in Loudon ; a clothier and captain ; removed from Loudon, N. H., to Rockland, Maine ; married Eliza Gleason in 1821. He died June 27, 1869, in Thomaston, Me., where he resided. She died in Thomaston, Me.

**42.** viii. ELISHA[5] PIPER (*Samuel[4]*, *Samuel[3]*, *Samuel[2]*, *Nathaniel[1]*), born Nov. 23, 1796, in Loudon ; died in May, 1862.

**43.** ix. ENOCH WOOD[5] PIPER (*Samuel[4]*, *Samuel[3]*, *Samuel[2]*, *Nathaniel[1]*), born Aug. 23, 1799, in Loudon ; died.

(**19.**) Comfort[4] Piper married Joseph Norris.

THEIR CHILDREN :

**44.** i. MEHITABLE[5] NORRIS (*Comfort[4]*, *Samuel[3]*, *Samuel[2]*, *Nathaniel[1]*), born Feb. 21, 1775, in Stratham, N. H.; died.

**45.** ii. JAMES[5] NORRIS (*Comfort[4]*, *Samuel[3]*, *Samuel[2]*, *Nathaniel[1]*), born Jan. 31, 1778, in Stratham ; died.

**46.** iii. JOSEPH[5] NORRIS (*Comfort[4]*, *Samuel[3]*, *Samuel[2]*, *Nathaniel[1]*,) born Nov. 5, 1779, in Stratham ; died.

*SAMUEL[5] PIPER'S CHILDREN :
1. Alonzo[6], born March 14, 1822 ; died young. 2. Sarah Jane[6], born Oct. 25, 1825 ; married James Stickney, of Lowell, Mass. She died June 4, 1852. 3. George[6], born Sept. 20, 1827 ; died Feb. 22, 1828. 4. Maria[6], born June 2, 1832, married James Stickney, of Lowell, Mass. as his second wife. 5. Elisha[6], born Oct. 8, 1834, married Georgia A. Nutter, of Pittsfield, N. H. He resides in Loudon. 6. Stephen B[6]., born March 28, 1837 ; married Sarah Berry, of Pittsfield, N. H. 7. Samuel[6], born March 26, 1839 ; died young.

† DAVID NORRIS[5] PIPER'S CHILDREN :
1. Aaron Gleason[6], born Feb. 27, 1820, in Thomaston, Me. ; married Eliza L. Young Aug., 1857. He died July 12, 1886. 2. Sarah Jane[6], born Dec. 3, 1823, in Thomaston ; married, 1st, Nelson S. Fales Nov., 1848 ; 2d, G. C. Dow July, 1862. 3. Mary Elizabeth[6], born Jan. 7, 1826, in Thomaston ; married Barnabas Webb Sept., 1848. They reside in Concord, California. 4. Martha Frances[6], born March 20, 1828, in Thomaston ; married George W. Beveredge Jan. 11, 1846. She died April 24, 1864, in Thomaston. 5. David Norris[6], born Jan. 26, 1831, in Thomaston, Me., where he now resides.

**47.** iv. BENJAMIN⁵ NORRIS (*Comfort⁴, Samuel³, Samuel², Nathaniel¹*), born Aug. 31, 1781, in Stratham ; died.

**48.** v. MARY⁵ NORRIS (*Comfort⁴, Samuel³, Samuel², Nathaniel¹*), born Nov. 11, 1784, in Stratham ; died.

**49.** vi. CHARLES⁵ NORRIS (*Comfort⁴, Samuel³, Samuel², Nathaniel¹*), born June 22, 1786, in Stratham ; died.

**50.** vii. NANCY⁵ NORRIS (*Comfort⁴, Samuel³, Samuel², Nathaniel¹*), born July 30, 1788, in Stratham ; died.

**51.** viii. NATHANIEL⁵ NORRIS (*Comfort⁴, Samuel³, Samuel², Nathaniel¹*), born April 14, 1791, in Stratham ; died.

**52.** ix. CALEB W⁵. NORRIS (*Comfort⁴, Samuel³, Samuel², Nathaniel¹*), born Nov. 8, 1792, in Stratham ; died.

(**20.**) Elisha⁴ Piper married, 1st, Sarah Barker ; 2d, Olive Dyer ; 3d, Rosannah Dyer.

THEIR CHILDREN :

**53.** i. SUKY⁵ PIPER (*Elisha⁴, Samuel³, Samuel², Nathaniel¹*), born Feb. 15, 1767, in Stratham, N. H.   In her publishment and her father's will, her name is Susanna.  I have given it as found in the family record, as I have given the names of the other children.   She married James Remick Aug. 30, 1788, born about 1764, in Kittery, Me.; a farmer, blacksmith, and justice of the peace. She died about Feb. 28, 1791, perhaps a few days later, in Parsonsfield, Me., at the birth of her second daughter, at the early age of twenty-four years.   His second wife was Anna Haynes, born in 1764, in Waterborough, Me.; died April 8, 1848, in Bangor, Me., where she resided with her step-daughter, Susan (Remick) Clarke. He resided in Parsonsfield on the south side of the North Road, about half way between Blazo's Corner and Limerick Village, on the farm now owned by Samuel Bartlett, being lot No. 171 and nearly opposite the residence of the late Samuel Lougee.   He was a large, portly man ; died July 31, 1822, in Parsonsfield.   I have not been able to ascertain the exact time when he was born or she died, but the time given varies very little from the true dates.   They were both buried in the burying-ground on the Moses Mighels farm, on the north side of the road, near where they resided.*—SEE THEIR CHILDREN : Nos. **63. 64.**

* The facts given above were obtained mostly from William Bean, of Denmark, Me., who lived with Esquire Remick nine years, and was there when he died.

**54.** ii. BENJAMIN[5] PIPER (*Elisha[4]*, *Samuel[3]*, *Samuel[2]*, *Nathaniel[1]*), born Aug. 19, 1769, in Stratham ; a farmer ; married Hannah Hodgdon, born in 1770, in Limerick, Me.   He died April 15, 1803, in Parsonsfield, Me., of pneumonia, from exposure by standing in the snow, without exercise, at town-meeting on the fourth of the same month, the unparalleled quantity of one foot having fallen the previous day.   She died April 12, 1849, in Parsonsfield, aged 79 years.   He resided in Parsonsfield on the South Road.—SEE THEIR CHILDREN : NOS. **65, 66, 67, 68.**

**55.** iii. DAVID[5] PIPER (*Elisha[4]*, *Samuel[3]*, *Samuel[2]*, *Nathaniel[1]*), born Dec. 24, 1771, in Stratham, N. H.; a ship-builder, brickmaker, and farmer ; married Nancy Chevers* May 23, 1793, born Sept. 16, 1776, in Salem, Mass.   After his marriage he settled in Hampden, Me., and was engaged in ship-building in company with another man, in 1814, when the British, on the third of Sept. of that year, made an attack on the town, pillaged the houses and stores, and burned several vessels which were in course of construction, one of which belonged to him and his partner.   After a battle of one hour the British were victorious, and according to "Coolidge and Mansfield's History of New England," carried away to Castine, Me., about eighty of the citizens as prisoners of war, of whom he was one ; only fifty-seven appear on the parole.   They were, however, soon released on the condition that the selectmen of Hampden should pay one thousand dollars as a ransom ; but the war soon closing, and the treaty of peace having been ratified at Washington Feb. 17, 1815, the money was never paid.   A copy of the parole of the prisoners is now in the possession of his grand-daughter, Mrs. Mary T.[7] (Jemegan) McGill, of Amelia, Ohio, who has had the kindness to furnish me a copy†.   The great loss of property occa-

---

* There has been some doubt about this name, but it is recorded in the marriage records of the town of Parsonsfield, Me., Nancy Chevers.

† COPY OF THE PAROLE WITH THE NAMES OF THE PRISONERS OF WAR : Samuel Webster, Josiah Ward, Eben Atwood, Archibald York, Truman Dean, Pangs Young, Solomon Covill, Jonathan Hopkins, John Smith, Abraham Knowles, Nathaniel Moysper, Isaac Hopkins, John Phillips, Jason Simpson, Benjamin Walker, Charles Page, Jessy Libby, Jr., Samuel H. Scott, Richard Ellingwood, Henry Smith, Benjamin Higgins, Henry Snow, Joel Hopkins, Rich. Stubbs, Eben Stubbs, Robert Daing, William Snow, Seth Higgins, Daniel Deane, Micajah Snow, Jeremiah Simpson, Lt. of Infantry, Abisha Higgins, Barnabas Atwood, Dawson Lined, Amos Deane, Jr., Solomon Myrick, Barker Turner, Truman Snow,

sioned by the destruction of his vessel, and the complete prostration
of business at the close of the war, in connection with the cold years
of 1815 and 1816*, caused his financial ruin, and he resolved to em-
igrate to the West, and try his fortune there.   Some time in  1817
he went to Ohio, and settled in New Richmond, Clermont County.
After remaining there a year, and making the necessary prepara-
tions, his son-in-law, Hiram Harding, in 1818, moved his family and
his own, consisting of ten persons in all, to that place, traveling all
that long and tedious journey of twelve hundred miles  in  a  wagon
covered with canvas, and drawn by two horses.   In many places
the roads were so soft and muddy that all, except the smallest children, were obliged to walk, many a mile on foot.   They all, however, arrived safely.   He lived in New Richmond about eleven years,
or till 1828, and was engaged in farming and brick-making, and
made the first bricks ever made in New Richmond.   He removed
from this place to Cincinnatti, and carried on brick-making there
for three years, when he purchased a farm at Pleasant Hill, a place
about four miles from Amelia, Ohio, and pursued the business of farming about six years, and made considerable money.   He then sold
this farm, and purchased another in Amelia, to which he removed
and continued the business of farming till his death, which occurred

*David Piper*, Jeremiah Baker, Elias Dudly, Adj. Bath Cav'y, Peter
Newcomb, Capt. 3d 10th Division, Jacob Nelson, Lieut. of the Cavalry,
Stephen Dollour, Ensign, Allen Rogers, Joshua Shannon, Benjamin
Swett, Simeon Mayo, Amos Rider, Joseph Mayo, Ezra Mayo, James
Mayo, Moses Baker, Thos. Mayo, Eben Young, Jr., William Higgins,
Samuel Hambleton.

The above names, prisoners of war, are hereby paroled upon honor not
to serve and take up arms directly or indirectly against Great Britain or
her allies during existing hostilities with America until regularly ex-
changed, to which engagement they have pledged themselves by a written document.

G. GOSSILIN, *B. G. Com't.*

Castine, 13th Sept., 1814.

The within is a true copy of a document in our possession.

ATTEST: SIMEON STETSON, }   *Selectmen of the*
JONA. KNOWLES, \ *Town of Hampden.*

Hampden, Sept. 20, 1814.

*During the summer of 1816 there was a killing frost in Maine every
month, which has never happened since   General Chamberlain, in his
work, "Maine: Her Place in History," says that in 1815 and 1816 "the
State lost fifteen thousand of her most energetic people."   This great
exodus was sometimes called the Ohio fever.

at that place Dec. 10, 1861, at the age of almost ninety years.
His wife died Sept. 27, 1852, in Amelia. He was a man of high
integrity, and respected by those who knew him. In person he was
tall and erect, being fully six feet in height, and capable of great
endurance. He visited his early home in Parsonsfield, in 1826,
which was the only time after he went to Ohio. Notwithstanding
his reverses he made life a success, and accumulated a good property which, at his death, was equally divided among his children.—
SEE THEIR CHILDREN : Nos. **69, 70, 71, 72.**

**56.** iv. SARAH⁵ PIPER (*Elisha⁴, Samuel³, Samuel², Nathaniel¹*),
usually called Sally, born March 17, 1774, in Wakefield, N. H.;
married Daniel Felch, son of Abijah Felch*, born September 26,
1771, in Limerick, Me.; a merchant and captain. His store is said
to have been the first in that section of the country, or between the
two Ossipee Rivers. He pursued the business of trade with great
success, and accumulated a large property for a man dying so young.
He died Oct. 3, 1806, in Limerick, where he resided. She died
Feb. 28, 1808, in the same place, a little more than a year after.
By the early death of the parents, the children were scattered, and
never again united in one household ; but all except one arrived at
maturity, married, and had children ; and became the most distinguished branch of the Piper family.—SEE THEIR CHILDREN : Nos. **73,
74, 75, 76, 77, 78.**

**57.** v. DANIEL⁵ PIPER (*Elisha⁴, (Samuel³, Samuel², Nathaniel¹*),
born March 4, 1776, in Wakefield, N. H.; a farmer, selectman, and
ensign in the war of 1812 ; married Anna Parsons Aug. 25, 1799,
born May 7, 1783, in Parsonsfield, Me., and daughter of Thomas
and Hannah (Foster) Parsons. Thomas Parsons was son of Thomas
Parsons, the proprietor of Parsonsfield, from whom the town took its
name. The "History of Penobscot County" says : "Mr. Piper came
to this county from Parsonsfield in 1799, and settled in Newburgh,
being one of the early settlers of the town. He was for many years
one of the active men of his town, holding all the prominent town
offices, at different times," and was in the battle of Hampden, being ensign under Captain Ichabod Bickford. He was a little above

---

* Abijah Felch was one of the early proprietors of the land of the township of Limerick, and a prominent man there for many years. He represented the town in the Massachusetts Legislature, in Boston, before
Maine was separated from that State in 1820. He also served in the army
of the Revolution.

the medium size, of high integrity, and decided in his opinions.
In religious belief, he was a Freewill Baptist.    He died August
10, 1842, in Newburgh, where he had always lived after his settlement there.    His wife died Oct. 5, 1865, in Monroe, Me., where
she was living with her son, Simeon Barker[5] Piper.    The date of
her death given in the town records of Newburgh is Nov. 1, 1865,
but her son says the one here given is correct.—SEE THEIR CHIL-
DREN : Nos. **79, 80, 81, 82, 83, 84, 85, 86, 87, 88, 89,
90.**

   **58.** vi. MARY[5] PIPER (*Elisha[4], Samuel[3], Samuel[2], Nathaniel[1]*),
usually called Polly, born April 14, 1778, in Wakefield, N. H.;
married Joseph Moffatt in 1796, born Sept. 4, 1771, in Maine, as is
supposed. but it may have been in Mass.    He became acquainted
with his wife at her father's residence in Parsonsfield, Me., while
employed by him on his farm.    After his marriage he settled on lot
No. 5, in Newburgh, Me., the town then being called Plantation
No. 2, where he lived several years, sowed a nursery, and made
other improvements.    In 1805, he sold his farm to George Bickford,
and it is now owned by his son, Isaac Bickford, who is nearly ninety years old[*].    He remembers the family well, and from him I have
obtained a part of the facts here given, and a portion of the remainder from the records of the town of Newburgh.    We have no certain
knowledge of his location after he sold his farm, till we find him in
Canada on a farm near Quebec, where his son, Benjamin Franklin
Moffatt, was born Oct. 8, 1815.    Mr. Bickford thinks that he resided in Newburgh, or some neighboring town, for several years after
he sold his farm.    Some of his grandchildren are of opinion that he
also lived a short time in some town in Mass., near Boston, before
he went to Canada.    From Canada he removed to Olean, Cattarau-
gus County, N. Y., probably about 1817, and in 1818, or the spring
of 1819 went to Ohio, and settled on a farm located between Hamilton and Oxford, in Butler County.    He made the passage from
Olean to Cincinnatti, Ohio, with his family on a raft loaded with
lumber, going 300 miles on the Alleghany River to Pittsburgh, Pa.,
and then 480 on the Ohio to Cincinnatti, the whole distance being
nearly 800 miles, and the time occupied, six weeks.    He lived on
this farm till 1823.    His wife died there in Dec., 1822, of measles,
contracted from the children, while he was absent in Illinois in

---

[*] He died April 11, 1889, a few months after this was written, being
born May 26, 1799.

search of a farm for a new residence. Nearly all the family were
sick at the same time, but all survived except the mother. She was
buried in the burying-ground on the farm. She was an active woman, and an excellent manager. The next spring, in 1823, he removed his family to a farm near Peoria, Ill., which he had selected
the previous year. He resided here till the latter part of his life,
when he went to live with his daughter, Olive (Moffatt) Proctor, and
her husband Abel Proctor, at Scales Mound, Ill. He died there
Feb. 10, 1850. at the age of 78 years. He was an upright and very
industrious man.—SEE THEIR CHILDREN : Nos. **91, 92, 93, 94,
95, 96, 97, 98, 99, 100, 101.**

**59.** vii. ELISHA[5] PIPER (*Elisha[4], Samuel[3], Samuel[2], Nathaniel[1]*),
born May 1, 1781, in Parsonsfield, Me.; a farmer; married Betsey
Mighels*, born Jan. 29, 1773, in Newmarket, N. H., being older
than her husband. He died of fever Oct., 1812, in Newburgh, Me.,
where he first settled. She died Aug. 15, 1864, in Newburgh, aged
91 years.—SEE THEIR CHILDREN : Nos. **102, 103, 104, 105,
106, 107, 108.**

**60.** viii. JANE[5] PIPER (*Elisha[4], Samuel[3], Samuel[2], Nathaniel[1]*),
born May 1, 1783, in Parsonsfield, Me.: married Jacob Bradbury,
June 20, 1803, born Jan. 7, 1769, in Biddeford, Me.: a farmer.
He was an active man and a good farmer. He died May 4, 1837,
in Limerick, Me. She died Oct. 2, 1863, in Limerick. She was a
woman a little above the medium size, of an amiable disposition, with
black eyes and dark hair. He resided in Limerick, near Felch's
Corner.—SEE THEIR CHILDREN : Nos. **109, 110, 111, 112, 113.**

**61.** ix. BETSEY[5] PIPER (*Elisha[4], Samuel[3], Samuel[2], Nathaniel[1]*),
born April 11, 1786, in Parsonsfield, Me.; married Isaac Felch, son
of Abijah Felch, in 1805, born in Limerick, Me., May 7, 1782 ; a
farmer, selectman, trustee of Parsonsfield Seminary, and lieutenant.
After his marriage he lived in Limerick several years, but in 1816
removed to Parsonsfield on a farm near the Seminary, where he lived
many years as a successful farmer. In 1836 he sold his farm, and
removed to Gorham, Me., where he died June 14, 1841. His wife
died Oct. 3, 1841, in Gorham. She was a woman of medium size,
with blue eyes and dark hair ; of active temperament and very in-

---

* This name was originally Mighel, but most of the family now spell it
Mighels, and almost all the people pronounce it so. Dr. Jesse Mighel
and Rev. Moses Mighel Smart, who have investigated the subject, spelled
it Mighel.

dustrious.—SEE THEIR CHILDREN: Nos. **114, 115, 116, 117, 118, 119, 120.**

**62.** X. JONATHAN⁵ PIPER (*Elisha⁴, Samuel³, Samuel², Nathaniel¹*), born Dec. 30, 1788, in Parsonsfield, Me.; a farmer, teacher, school committee, selectman, land-surveyor, justice of the peace, county commissioner, and one of the surveyors appointed to establish the boundary line between Maine and New Hampshire. He was in public business a large portion of his time for more than twenty years. He had a good common school and academical education, and in 1801 attended Fryeburg Academy, at Fryeburg, Me., for some time, and was under the instruction of Daniel Webster, who was Principal of the institution at that time, and subsequently became so distinguished as a lawyer, orator, and statesman. In politics he was a Whig, and subsequently a Republican. He was several times a candidate for representative to the State Legislature, and had the full vote of his party ; but as there were about twice as many Democrats in town as Whigs, he was not elected. No Whig was elected by the town as representative to the Legislature during his political career. He had a taste for music, could read it readily, and sung regularly in the church choir for many years. On the tenor drum he was a first-class player, and drum-major of his regiment. His open beat and full roll and his imitation of a battle scene, with the continuous and heavy roll of the drum and the discharge of musketry in volleys and irregular shots, were very fine. He married Mary Burbank, usually called Polly, March 15, 1810, daughter of Capt. Silas and Hannah (Baird) Burbank*, born in Scarborough, Me., Aug. 6, 1788. She

---

* Capt. Silas Burbank was born in Massachusetts, and died Sept., 1814, at his residence in Parsonsfield, Me., being in the 70th year of his age. His family consisted of five sons and four daughters: Eleazer married Anna Brackett ; Silas married Sally Wedgwood ; David married Miriam Dunnells ; Samuel married Esther Boothby ; Caleb, unmarried ; Abigail married Silas Harmon ; Betsey married Solomon Hodgdon ; Hannah married Capt. Tristram Redman ; and Mary married Jonathan Piper, as above. At the breaking out of the War of the Revolution, he raised a company of soldiers in Scarborough, Me., where he then resided, and being made captain, marched to Boston. Mass., and joined the Continental Army. His two young sons, Silas, then 17 years of age, and David 15, were the musicians, the former being the drummer, and the latter the fifer. He served through the war, participating in some of the most important battles of that great struggle. He was at one time captain of Washington's life-guard, and permitted to sit at the table with him and his higher officers. One day at dinner, when Washington began to wait

was a faithful mother, of a kind and cheerful disposition, and of true
Christian character; and always instilled into the minds of her children high moral and religious principles. She died suddenly of
heart-disease July 14, 1873, in Parsonsfield, only three days after
the death of her husband. He always resided in Parsonsfield, first
on the South Road where all his children were born. The house
was located on the south side of the road, opposite the residence of
his father. It has been removed recently, but the place where it
stood can be easily identified, being at the eastern base of the hill on
which is the new cemetery. He sold his farm on the South Road,
and removed to the north part of the town, near Parsonsfield Seminary, on the farm previously owned by his brother-in-law, Isaac
Felch, which he purchased of him in 1836. In person he was a little below the medium size, decided in his opinions, and quick and
accurate in all his business transactions. He was of high integrity,
and gained the confidence and respect of those with whom he asso-
ciated. He died July 11, 1873, in Parsonsfield, where he resided.
—SEE THEIR CHILDREN : Nos. **121, 122, 123, 124.**

### SIXTH GENERATION.

(**53.**) Suky[5] Piper married James Remick.

#### THEIR CHILDREN :

**63.** i. JANE[6] REMICK (*Suky*[5], *Elisha*[4], *Samuel*[3], *Samuel*[2], *Nathan-
el*[1]), born in 1789, in Parsonsfield, Me.; married Thomas Caril,
Sept. 18, 1811, born in 1784, in Waterborough, Me.; a timber-dealer,
lumber-manufacturer, and representative in the Maine Legislature.
She died at Union Falls, in Hollis (now Dayton), where they then
resided, Sept. 29, 1829, aged 40 years. He afterward married Susan Felch[6], cousin of his first wife, and removed to Salmon Falls,
Hollis, Me.

**64.** ii. SUSAN[6] REMICK (*Suky*[5], *Elisha*[4], *Samuel*[3], *Samuel*[2], *Nathaniel*[1]), born Feb. 28, 1791, in Parsonsfield, Me.; married Royal

upon the table, he filled a plate, and handed it to him first. He was sur-
prised, blushed, hesitated, but finally took it. After he had recovered his
self-possession, he began to think why Washington waited upon him first.
He came to the conclusion that he looked eagerly at the food on the table
(it being a boiled dinner of which he was very fond, and he was also very
hungry, having been on duty the previous night, and had no breakfast)
and that Washington observed it, and his tender care for his soldiers,
prompted him to wait upon him before his higher officers, who had their
regular meals. He loved Washington as a father, and often tears would
start in his eyes at the mention of his name.

Clarke, of Cornish, Me., March 29, 1809, born in 1783, in Epping,
N. H.; a deacon of the Calvin Baptist Church, trustee of Colby University, and high sheriff of Penobscot County.  He died Dec. 5, 1858,
in Bangor, aged 75 years.   She died Nov. 19, 1866, in Bangor,
where they resided, aged 75 years.   The following notice of her appeared in the " Zion's Advocate :"  " Susan (Remick) Clarke was an
estimable Christian woman, of great force of character, and of more
than ordinary intelligence."*

(54.) Benjamin[3] Piper married Hannah Hodgdon.

THEIR CHILDREN :

**63.** i. ELISHA[6] PIPER *(Benjamin[5], Elisha[4], Samuel[3], Samuel[2],
Nathaniel[1])*, born Jan. 22, 1796, in Parsonsfield, Me.; a farmer
and carpenter : married Sally Foster, born Aug. 21, 1812, in Parsonsfield ; died there Dec. 24, 1869.   He was a man of great industry, of high moral principles, and respected by all who knew him.
He founded Parsonsfield Free High School with an endowment of
eleven thousand and fifty-six dollars.   He also gave the Methodist
Church, in Newfield, Me., where he was at that time residing, a fine
church bell, costing three hundred and fifty dollars, and weighing
nine hundred pounds.   He was reared a Freewill Baptist, and always attended that church when he lived in his native town ; he was
not, however, confined to any particular religious denomination in
his gifts, but bestowed them wherever he thought they would do the
most good.   He was a constant attendant on religious services on
the Sabbath, and contributed a liberal proportion for the support of
the ministry.   He resided the most of his life on the old homestead
of his father, on the South Road in Parsonsfield.   He died March
22, 1877, in Parsonsfield.   They had no children.

**66.** ii. SALLY[6] PIPER *(Benjamin[5], Elisha[4], Samuel[3], Samuel[2],
Nathaniel[1])*, born about Sept. 10, 1797, in Parsonsfield, Me.; mar-
ried Isaac Moore, born March 5, 1788, in Parsonsfield ; a farmer.
She died July 10, 1835, in Parsonsfield, aged 37 years and 10 months.
He died May 6, 1841, in Parsonsfield, where he resided.—SEE THEIR
CHILDREN : Nos. **125. 126. 127. 128. 129. 130. 131. 132.**

**67.** iii. POLLY[6] PIPER *(Benjamin[5], Elisha[4], Samuel[3], Samuel[2],
Nathaniel[1])*, born Jan. 9, 1800, in Parsonsfield, Me.; married Gid-

* They had several daughters, one of whom, Anna Judson, born Feb.
14, 1819, married Rev. Joseph Ricker, D. D., born June 27, 1814, in Parsonsfield, and now residing in Augusta, Me.   She died Nov. 16, 1847.

con Bickford, born Jan. 12, 1796, in Parsonsfield; a farmer, captain of Parsonsfield Light Infantry, and deputy sheriff. After his marriage he first settled on the South Road in Parsonsfield, but subsequently removed to the Hathaway place, in the north part of the town, where he resided many years. A few years before his death he sold his farm, and purchased the Dame place on the North Road, where he died Feb. 3, 1873, aged seventy-seven years. She died March 20, 1882, in Monmouth, Me., aged eighty-two years, two months, and eleven days. He was a successful farmer.—SEE THEIR CHILDREN : Nos. **133, 134, 135, 136, 137, 138, 139, 140, 141, 142, 143.**

**68.** IV. BENJAMIN[5] PIPER (*Benjamin[5], Elisha[4], Samuel[3], Samuel[2], Nathaniel[1]*), born March 29, 1802, in Parsonsfield, Me.; a farmer; married, 1st, Nancy Sargent, born Nov. 9, 1808; died Jan. 24, 1870, in Parsonsfield; 2d, Mercy Smith, Oct. 28, 1872 (maiden name Mercy Lang, widow of David Smith, of Limerick, Me.), born Feb. 24, 1805, in Effingham, N. H. He died Dec. 23, 1881, in Newfield, Me. After his first marriage he resided, first, in Shapleigh, Me., then in Parsonsfield, and lastly in Newfield, Me. He was a successful farmer.—SEE THEIR CHILDREN : Nos. **144, 145, 146, 147, 148.**

(**55.**) David[5] Piper married Nancy Chevers.

THEIR CHILDREN :

**69.** i. LAVINIA[6] PIPER (*David[5], Elisha[4], Samuel[3], Samuel[2], Nathaniel[1]*), born Oct. 22, 1794, in Hampden, Me.; married Hiram Harding Feb. 16, 1815, born Aug. 2, 1790, in Medway, Mass.; a farmer and boatman. He died March 27, 1827, by drowning in the Ohio River about midway between New Richmond, Ohio, and Cincinnatti, Ohio. She died Oct. 9, 1871, in Bloomington, Ill., where she was living with her daughter, Lavinia (Harding) White and son-in-law, David E. White. He resided at New Richmond at the time of his death.—SEE THEIR CHILDREN : Nos. **149, 150, 151, 152, 153.**

**70.** ii. EZEKIEL[6] PIPER (*David[5], Elisha[4], Samuel[3], Samuel[2], Nathaniel[1]*), born Dec. 27, 1795, in Hampden, Me.; a farmer; married Ann Roberts, born July 17, 1797, in Bucks County, Pa. She died Feb. 6, 1871, in Hollowayville, Ill. He died Dec. 30, 1875, in Malden, Ill. After the death of his wife he removed to Malden. He was a successful farmer.—SEE THEIR CHILDREN : Nos. **154, 155, 156, 157, 158, 159, 160.**

**71.** iii. ELISHA[6] PIPER (*David[5]*, *Elisha[4]*, (*Samuel[3]*, *Samuel[2]*, *Nathaniel[1]*), born April 4, 1799, in Hampden, Me.; a farmer and brickmaker; married Ann Lewis, Oct. 25, 1824, born July 2. 1800, in Pa. He died July 16, 1841, in Leepertown, Ill., where he resided. She died Nov. 25, 1869, in Selby, Ill., to which place she removed after the death of her husband.—SEE THEIR CHILDREN : Nos. **161, 162, 163, 164, 165, 166, 167.**

**72.** iv. NANCY FROTHINGHAM[6] PIPER (*David[5]*, *Elisha[4]*, *Samuel[3]*, *Samuel[2]*, *Nathaniel[1]*), born Aug. 2, 1809, in Hampden, Me.; married David Jernegan Sept. 24, 1829, born Dec. 7, 1806, in Martha's Vineyard, Mass.; a wool-carder and merchant. She died Dec. 30, 1880, in Amelia, Ohio. He died Aug. 3, 1885, at Amelia, where he resided.—SEE THEIR CHILDREN : Nos. **168, 169.**

(**58.**) Sarah[5] Piper married Daniel Felch.

THEIR CHILDREN :

**73.** i. SUSAN PIPER[6] FELCH (*Sarah[5]*, *Elisha[4]*, *Samuel[3]*, *Samuel[2]*, *Nathaniel[1]*), born May 23, 1797, in Limerick, Me.; a teacher before marriage ; married John Felch, born Jan. 1, 1795, in Limerick ; a farmer and merchant. He first resided in Limerick, being engaged in trade for several years, and then removed to New Limerick, Me.. and pursued the business of farming. His wife died Nov. 28, 1853, in New Limerick. After her death he went to Livonia, Minn., and died there May 20, 1870.

**74.** ii. SARAH BARKER[6] FELCH (*Sarah[5]*, *Elisha[4]*, *Samuel[3]*, *Samuel[2]*, *Nathaniel[1]*), born in 1798, in Limerick, Me.; married Caleb Fessenden Page, born in 1798, in Fryeburg, Me.; a Congregational clergyman ; graduated at Bowdoin College in 1820, and studied theology with Rev. David Thurston, of Winthrop, Me. He was pastor of the Congregational Church in Limington, Me., ten years; Bridgeton, Me., eighteen ; Granby, Ct., five ; Granville, Mass., five ; Tolland, Mass., three ; Colebrook, N. H., four ; and Milton Mills, N. H., eight. After a long career of usefulness in his profession, he died at Milton Mills Nov. 6, 1873, at the age of seventy-five years. His wife was educated at Limerick Academy, Limerick, Me., and was an accomplished lady, worthy of the important position which she occupied. She died May 24, 1839, in Bridgeton, Me., where they then resided, aged forty-one years.

**75.** iii. LYDIA[6] FELCH (*Sarah[5]*, *Elisha[4]*, *Samuel[3]*, *Samuel[2]*, *Nathaniel[1]*), born May 8, 1800, in Limerick, Me.; married Simeon Lougee Dec. 12, 1816, born Jan. 9, 1795, in Parsonsfield, Me.; a

mechanic and farmer. He resided several years in Limerick near Felch's Corner, working at his trade and on his farm; but subsequently removed to New Limerick, Me., and continued to pursue the business of farming. He died Sept. 9, 1874, in New Limerick. She died Nov. 6, 1877, in New Limerick, where they resided.

**76.** iv. JULIA[6] FELCH (*Sarah[5]*, *Elisha[4]*, *Samuel[3]*, *Samuel[2]*, *Nathaniel[1]*), born July 31, 1802, in Limerick, Me.; married James Hopkinson March 20, 1821, born May 28, 1794, in Saco, Me.; a farmer, timber-dealer, and lumber-manufacturer. He carried on the lumbering business at Union Falls in Hollis (now Dayton), Me. He owned a fine farm in Saco, where he was engaged in farming also. She died Oct. 16, 1845, in Saco. He died Feb. 18, 1854, in Saco, where he then resided.

**77.** v. ALPHEUS[6] FELCH (*Sarah[5]*, *Elisha[4]*, *Samuel[3]*, *Samuel[2]*, *Nathaniel[1]*), born Sept. 28, 1804,* in Limerick, Me.; graduated at Bowdoin College in 1827, entered immediately upon the study of law, and was admitted to the bar at Bangor, Me., in 1830. He first began to practice in Holton, Me., where he remained three years, from 1830 to 1833. His health having become impaired by the severity of the climate, and desiring a more promising locality for business, he removed to Monroe, Michigan, where he resided ten years, or till 1843, and then settled at Ann Arbor, in the same State, where he has continued to practice his profession to the present time. He has held various offices of trust and honor; has been representative in the Legislature of Michigan, Bank Commissioner, Commissioner of California Land Claims, Tappan Professor of Law and President of the Board of Regents of the University of Michigan, Judge of the Supreme Court and Governor of Michigan, and United States Senator from 1847 to 1853. He discharged all these offices with much ability and honor to himself and his State. In 1877 Bowdoin College conferred on him the honorary degree of

* The date of his birth has sometimes appeared in print as being Sept. 28, 1806, but the one here given is correct, having been furnished me by himself. His children are as follows: 1. Caroline Ophelia, born Oct. 22, 1838. 2. Elizabeth Hopkinson, born March 20, 1841. 3. Emma Lucretia, born March 21, 1843; died Dec. 20, 1875. 4. Arthur Willis, born Feb. 15, 1845; died July 17, 1846. 5. Theodore Alpheus, born March 30, 1847. 6. Florence Cornelia, born Jan. 9, 1852; died Oct. 31, 1862. 7. Francis Lawrence, born Jan. 5, 1854. 8. Helen Louise, born Feb. 6, 1858. All were born in Ann Arbor, Michigan, except the first three, who were born in Monroe, Michigan. Those deceased died in Ann Arbor.

LL. D.  He married Lucretia Williams Lawrence Sept. 14, 1837.
an estimable lady, daughter of Judge Wolcott and Caroline (Steb-
bins) Lawrence, born Dec. 31, 1817, in Monroe, Mich.  She died
July 30, 1882, in Ann Arbor.  He resides in Ann Arbor.

**78.** vi.  EUNICE[6] FELCH (*Sarah[5]*, *Elisha[4]*, *Samuel[3]*, *Samuel[2]*, *Nathaniel[1]*), born about May 30, 1806, in Limerick, Me.; died Oct.
30, 1809, in Cornish, Me., aged three years and five months.  She
was buried in Limerick, in the cemetery near the Calvin Baptist meet-
ing-house, where her parents were buried.

(**57.**) Daniel[5] Piper married Anna Parsons.

THEIR CHILDREN :

**79.** i.  THOMAS PARSONS[6] PIPER ( *Daniel[5]*, *Elisha[4]*, *Samuel[3]*, *Samuel[2]*, *Nathaniel[1]*), born April 23, 1800, in Newburgh, Me. ; a farmer ;
married, 1st, Lucy Turner Gilman March 11, 1827, born Sept. 30,
1806, in Belfast, Me.; died Dec. 24, 1845, in Newburgh ; 2d, widow Abigail Burdick True (maiden name Abigail Burdick Lanpher),
May 30, 1846, born May 9, 1804, in Searsport, Me.; died April 4,
1872, in Belfast.  He died Dec. 26, 1871, in Belfast, where he resided.—SEE THEIR CHILDREN : Nos. **170, 171, 172.**

**80.** ii.  *Daniel[6]* PIPER ( *Daniel[5]*, *Elisha[4]*, *Samuel[3]*, *Samuel[2]*, *Nathaniel[1]*), born June 14, 1802, in Newburgh, Me.; died Jan. 19, 1810,
in Newburgh.

**81.** iii.  BENJAMIN[6] PIPER ( *Daniel[5]*, *Elisha[4]*, *Samuel[3]*. *Samuel[2]*,
*Nathaniel[1]*), born July 25, 1804, in Newburgh, Me.; a farmer ; married Julia Bickford Sept. 17, 1829, born May 5, 1812, in Newburgh.
He died of heart disease May 29, 1882, in Boston, Mass., while on
a visit to his daughter, Mrs. Evelyn Newcomb (Piper) Rutledge.
His residence was in Dixmont, Me.—SEE THEIR CHILDREN : Nos.
**173, 174, 175, 176, 177, 178, 179.**

**82.** iv.  ELISHA[6] PIPER (*Daniel[5]*, *Elisha[4]*, *Samuel[3]*, *Samuel[2]*, *Nathaniel[1]*), born Sept. 1, 1806, in Newburgh, Me.; a farmer ; married
Rhoda Hilton Blckford Aug. 28, 1831, born May 7, 1809, in Newburgh ; died Dec. 21, 1879, in Newburgh.  He resides in Newburgh.
—SEE THEIR CHILDREN : Nos. **180, 181, 182, 183, 184.**

**83.** v.  HANNAH FOSTER[6] PIPER (*Daniel[5]*, *Elisha[4]*, *Samuel[3]*, *Sam-
uel[2]*, *Nathaniel[1]*). born Nov. 16, 1808, in Newburgh, Me.; married
Elijah Bachelder Aug. 12, 1834, born Feb. 7, 1806, in Phipsburg,
Me.; a farmer.  He resided in Dixmont, Me., many years, but has

recently removed to Fairfield, Me.—SEE THEIR CHILDREN: Nos. **185, 186, 187, 188.**

**84.** vi. ABIGAIL HOBBS[6] PIPER (*Daniel[5], Elisha[4], Samuel[3], Samuel[2], Nathaniel[1]*), born Nov. 25, 1811, in Newburgh, Me.; died Dec. 25, 1838, in Newburgh.

**85.** vii. ENOCH PARSONS[6] PIPER (*Daniel[5], Elisha[4], Samuel[3], Samuel[2], Nathaniel[1]*), born July 1, 1814, in Newburgh, Me.; a carpenter; died Aug. 11, 1838, in Newburgh, where he resided.

**86.** viii. DANIEL[6] PIPER (*Daniel[5], Elisha[4], Samuel[3], Samuel[2], Nathaniel[1]*), a twin brother of Enoch Parsons[6], born July 1, 1814, in Newburgh, Me.; a farmer and selectman; married Hannah Foster Parsons, daughter of Enoch Poor and Betsey (Burnham) Parsons, July 16, 1837, born Sept. 14, 1808, in Parsonsfield, Me. She died June 7, 1883, in Parsonsfield. He settled in Parsonsfield in 1837, and has always resided there since that time.—SEE THEIR CHILD : No. **189.**

**87.** ix. SIMEON BARKER[6] PIPER, (*Daniel[5], Elisha[4], Samuel[3], Samuel[2], Nathaniel[1]*), born Dec. 2, 1816, in Newburgh, Me.; a carpenter; married, 1st. Hannah Kaylor in 1840, born in Baton Rouge, La.; died Dec. 1848, in New Orleans, La.; 2d. Harriet Augusta Wildes, daughter of Nathaniel and Anne Wildes, July 20, 1857, born Feb. 5, 1830, in Monroe, Me. He first settled in New Orleans, but now resides in Elizabeth, N. J.—SEE THEIR CHILDREN : Nos. **190, 191, 192, 193.**

**88.** x. ALPHEUS FELCH[6] PIPER (*Daniel[5], Elisha[4], Samuel[3], Samuel[2], Nathaniel[1]*), born Oct. 28, 1820, in Newburgh, Me.; a farmer and mill-wright; married, 1st. Catharine Smart Perkins March 27, 1843, born Aug. 10, 1826, in Palermo, Me.; died Nov. 11, 1843, in Newburgh : 2d. Susan Hannah Smith March 27, 1849, born Jan. 11, 1834, in Monroe, Me.; died Feb. 28, 1881, in Swanville, Me. He died Oct. 31, 1886, in Swanville. He first settled in Newburgh, and afterward in Swanville.—SEE THEIR CHILDREN : Nos **194, 195, 196, 197, 198.**

**89.** xi. JOHN USHER PARSONS[6] PIPER (*Daniel[5], Elisha[4], Samuel[3], Samuel[2], Nathaniel[1]*), born June 20, 1823, in Newburgh, Me.; a mechanic; married Elizabeth Packard Dec. 1844, born April 24, 1823, in Troy, Me. He died July 17, 1889, in Newburgh, where he resided.—SEE THEIR CHILDREN : Nos. **199, 200, 201.**

**90.** xii. DAVID[6] PIPER (*Daniel[5], Elisha[4], Samuel[3], Samuel[2], Na-

*thaniel¹*), born June 4, 1827, in Newburgh, Me.; a soldier in the war with Mexico; died Aug. 2, 1848, at Fortress Monroe, Va., on his return from Mexico.

(**58.**) Mary³ Piper married Joseph Moffatt.

THEIR CHILDREN :

**91.** i. ALVAH⁶ MOFFATT (*Mary³ Piper, Elisha⁴, Samuel³, Samuel², Nathaniel¹*), born Dec. 29, 1797, in Newburgh, Me.; a farmer and school trustee; married Clarissa Eades Feb. 11, 1823, born Dec. 19, 1805, in Virginia. He owned a large farm which he cultivated carefully. It contained a coal mine which he also worked profitably. In addition to his farm, he owned a large tract of land in the vicinity of Peoria, Ill., and became one of the most wealthy and prosperous farmers in his town. He was of a generous disposition, and gave liberally to those who needed assistance. In religion he was a Methodist. He died July 20, 1884, in Limestone, Ill., where he resided. His wife died March 16, 1884, in the same town.

**92.** ii. JOSEPH⁶ MOFFATT (*Mary³ Piper, Elisha⁴, Samuel³, Samuel², Nathaniel¹*), born in Newburgh, Me., about 1799; a farmer and lumberman. When about ten years of age he went to live with his grandfather, Elisha⁴ Piper, of Parsonsfield, Me., and remained with him till he was about fourteen, when he went to live with his father again. He was with him when the family went on the raft from Olean, N. Y., to Cincinnati, Ohio; and also on the farm near Hamilton, Butler County, Ohio. He died in 1822, a short time before his mother, on his return from New Orleans, La., where he had been with a boat-load of lumber for sale, and had contracted a fever. He was buried at "Mount Pulaski," in Pulaski County, Ill., probably a swell of land then called by that name, on the bank of the Ohio River, perhaps where Mound City now stands.

**93.** iii. ------⁶ MOFFATT (*Mary³ Piper, Elisha⁴, Samuel³, Samuel², Nathaniel¹*), born about 1801, in Newburgh, Me., and died there in infancy.

**94.** iv. AQUILA⁶ MOFFATT (*Mary³ Piper, Elisha⁴, Samuel³, Samuel², Nathaniel¹*), born March 19, 1802, in Newburgh, Me.; a farmer and school trustee; married, 1st, Matilda Jones March 9, 1832, born in Ohio; died in 1833, near Peoria, Ill.; 2d, Mary Bogardus (maiden name Mary Fowler) Dec. 4, 1834, born Jan. 4, 1805, in Connecticut; died July 27, 1873, near Peoria. He owned a

large farm which, like his brother Alvah's, contained a coal mine from which he derived a large profit. He also owned a large tract of land near Peoria. He was a Methodist, and took a deep interest in the Methodist Society where he lived, giving it a lot of land and a church which he built on it for the society's use as a place of worship. His house was large and convenient, and is said to have been almost a home for the Methodist ministers traveling in that section of the country. He died Jan. 10, 1880, on his farm near Peoria, in Peoria township, Ill., where he resided.

**95.** v. SARAH⁶ MOFFATT (*Mary⁵ Piper, Elisha⁴, Samuel³, Samuel², Nathaniel¹*), born Nov. 21, 1804, in Newburgh*, Me. After the death of her mother, when eighteen years of age, she left her paternal home, and went to provide for herself in Cincinnati, Ohio. After remaining there about a year she married Matthew Brown, Dec. 25, 1823, born in Keighley, Yorkshire, England, Oct. 17, 1806. He emigrated to this country with his father when only six years old, and was educated here. When twelve years of age he began to learn the trade of cabinet-maker, serving five years, and became a first-class workman. When General Lafayette visited this country, in 1824, he was selected by the reception committee of Cincinnati to make an elegant chair for him to sit in. The chair was of extraordinary workmanship, and is now carefully preserved with other interesting relics of the city. He followed the business of cabinet-making in Cincinnati about thirteen years, and then entered into trade, and by strict integrity and close attention to business, became a successful merchant. In the meantime, with much sagacity, he purchased real estate in the city, which rose largely on his hands, and he became quite wealthy. After diligent labor in trade for twenty years or more, he retired from business in 1854, retaining a portion of his real estate in the city, and purchased a country seat of ten acres at Delhi, about four and a half miles from Cincinnati, where he lived as a gentleman farmer and capitalist, with his family, to which he was much attached, in quiet leisure until his death, which occurred suddenly May 30, 1868, at Delhi. In politics he was a Republican, and took a deep interest in the suc-

---

*She told her children that she was born in "No. 2, Massachusetts." Maine was a part of Mass. till 1820. Newburgh, before its incorporation in 1819, was called Plantation No. 2, and was then a part of Mass. She was, therefore, correct in saying that she was born in "No. 2, Massachusetts."

cess of the Union Army in the War of the Rebellion. His wife died May 24, 1886, in Cincinnati, to which she and her surviving children* removed after the death of her husband. She was an active woman, of medium size with dark hair and black eyes, of amiable disposition, and highly respected.

**96.** vi. MARY[6] MOFFATT (*Mary*[5] *Piper, Elisha*[4], *Samuel*[3], *Samuel*[2], *Nathaniel*[1]). born July 21, 1806, probably in Newburgh, Me.; married Abel Proctor, Dec, 23, 1831, born March 31, 1800, in Vermont ; at first a printer, but subsequently a farmer. He lived on his farm at Scales Mound, Ill., for many years until sometime after the death of his wife, He then sold and purchased a tract of land for himself and children in Wright County, Iowa. He was a man of cultivated mind and high moral character. He died in Wright County, March 12, 1888, where he was residing with his daughter. His wife died May 14, 1865, at Scales Mound. Both were buried at Scales Mound.

**97.** vii. OLIVE[6] MOFFATT (*Mary*[5] *Piper, Elisha*[4], *Samuel*[3], *Samuel*[2], *Nathaniel*[1]). born Oct. 23. 1809, probably in Newburgh, Me.; married Samuel Scales, April 11, 1833, born in Rockingham County, North Carolina, April 17, 1805 ; a farmer, and extensive land-holder. He owned a farm containing over seven hundred acres near Shullsburgh, Wisconsin. and another large tract of land, rich in lead ore, near Scales Mound, Ill., which was named in honor of him. His mining lands rose to almost fabulous prices, and he became quite wealthy. All his purchases of land resulted favorably. He died Sept. 13, 1878, near White Oak Springs, Wis. His wife died July 18, 1845, in the same place.

**98.** viii. ELISHA[6] MOFFATT (*Mary*[5] *Piper, Elisha*[4], *Samuel*[3], *Samuel*[2], *Nathaniel*[1]), born about 1811, perhaps in Me.; died aged two years.

---

* Their children are as follows: 1. Mary Ann. born Dec. 3, 1824 : died Jan. 6, 1862. 2. Catharine, born Jan. 11, 1827. ; died Sept. 1, 1832. 3. Jane born March 23, 1829 ; died Aug, 25, 1829, 4. Joseph, born July 30, 1830 ; died July 10, 1832. 5. Matthew, born Nov. 16, 1832 ; died Feb. 16, 1836. 6. Clarissa, born Oct. 28, 1834 ; died Oct. 29, 1834. 7. Frances Olive, born Aug. 14, 1836 : died Dec. 18, 1874. 8. Sarah Euphemia, born July 7, 1838, living in Cincinnati. 9. Harriet Corwin, born Oct. 13, 1840, living in Cincinnati. She has rendered me valuable assistance in collecting genealogies for this book. See page 9. 10. Martha Ermina. born June 2, 1844 ; died Aug. 17, 1873. All were born in Cincinnati except Clarissa, who was born near Peoria, Illinois.

**99.** ix. ELIZA⁶ MOFFATT (*Mary⁵ Piper, Elisha⁴, Samuel³, Samuel², Nathaniel¹*), born about 1813. perhaps in Mass.; died in childhood.

**100.** x. BENJAMIN FRANKLIN⁶ MOFFATT (*Mary⁵ Piper, Elisha⁴, Samuel³, Samuel², Nathaniel¹*), born Oct. 8, 1815, near Quebec, Canada ; a farmer; married, 1st, Nancy Jane Risdon Jan., 1835, born in 1820 ; died Aug. 3, 1853, in Wisconsin ; 2d, Mercy Wayne (maiden name Mercy Rockwell), born in 1826, in Dayton, Ohio. He was a man of fine physical development, generous, and hospitable. He owned a good farm, but was not a land-holder. He died March 17, 1886, near Peoria, Ill., where he resided. His second wife resides in Lenora, Kansas.

**101.** xi. ——⁶ MOFFATT (*Mary⁵ Piper, Elisha⁴, Samuel³, Samuel², Nathaniel¹*), born about 1817, perhaps in Olean, N. Y.; died in infancy.

(59.) Elisha⁵ Piper married Betsey Mighels.

THEIR CHILDREN :

**102.** i. SALLY⁶ PIPER (*Elisha⁵, Elisha⁴, Samuel³, Samuel², Nathaniel¹*), born Sept. 24, 1799, in Parsonsfield, Me.; married Gideon Leavitt Oct., 1824, as his second wife, her sister Betsey having been his first, born May 10, 1793, in Newburgh, Me.; a farmer. He died Oct. 5, 1857, in Newburgh. She died Dec. 25, 1884, in Newburgh, where they resided.—SEE THEIR CHILDREN : Nos. **202, 203, 204, 205, 206, 207, 208, 209, 210, 211, 212.**

**103.** ii. BETSEY MIGHELS⁶ PIPER (*Elisha⁵, Elisha⁴, Samuel³, Samuel², Nathaniel¹*), born Aug. 9, 1801, in Newburgh, Me.; married Gideon Leavitt Feb. 11, 1820; born May 10, 1793, in Newburgh ; a farmer. She died March 22, 1824, in Newport, Me. He resided in Newport at the time of his wife's death, but afterward removed to Newburgh, and married her sister Sally.—SEE THEIR CHILDREN : Nos. **213, 214.**

**104.** iii. ANN⁶ PIPER (*Elisha⁵, Elisha⁴, Samuel³, Samuel², Nathaniel¹*), born May 16, 1803, in Newburgh, Me.; married George Bickford, son of Thomas and Nancy (Peace) Bickford, Sept. 1837 He was born June 9, 1802, in Newburgh ; a farmer ; died Sept. 3, 1880, in Newburgh, where he resided. She is now living (1889) at the age of eighty-six years, the fond mother of a large and respectable family of children, two of whom are college educated, and holding responsible positions in society.—SEE THEIR CHILDREN : Nos. **215, 216, 217, 218, 219, 220, 221, 222.**

**105.** iv. ELISHA⁶ PIPER (*Elisha⁵, Elisha⁴, Samuel³, Samuel², Nathaniel¹*), born Feb. 10, 1805, in Newburgh, Me.; died in August, 1805, in Newburgh.

**106.** v. DAVID⁶ PIPER (*Elisha⁵, Elisha⁴, Samuel³, Samuel², Nathaniel¹*), born May 11, 1807, in Newburgh, Me.; a farmer; died of consumption Oct., 1826, in Newburgh, Me., where he lived.

**107.** vi. ELISHA⁶ PIPER (*Elisha⁵, Elisha⁴, Samuel³, Samuel², Nathaniel¹*), born April 8, 1809, in Newburgh, Me.; a farmer; married Harriet Burbank, daughter of Ensign Samuel and Esther (Boothby) Burbank, Nov. 21, 1833, born Jan. 15, 1811, in Parsonsfield, Me. She was noted for her good scholarship when a schoolgirl, and now for the good management of her household affairs. She takes a deep interest in passing events and the progress of society. He resided on the old homestead devised to him by his grandfather, Elisha⁴ Piper, with whom he had lived from early childhood, and whose confidence and esteem he had gained by his fidelity, industry, and integrity. He was one of the largest and best farmers in town. In the management of his farm he followed in the footsteps of his grandfather, and conducted it with equal energy and success. He was acquainted with music, played the fife, and was chorister of the church choir for eighteen years. He was a Freewill Baptist in religious belief and by profession, and so are all his family. He died of pneumonia April 11, 1876, in Parsonsfield, where he resided.—SEE THEIR CHILDREN : Nos. **223, 224, 225.**

**168.** vii. JESSE⁶ PIPER (*Elisha⁵, Elisha⁴, Samuel³, Samuel², Nathaniel¹*), born March 9, 1811, in Newburgh, Me.; died May 18, 1827, on the homestead of his father, in Newburgh. On the day of his death he and another young man, by the name of Albert Nash, were planting corn, and during a thunder-shower took shelter from the rain under the body of a large tree which had been broken off by the wind and fallen nearly down, leaving a long splintery stump to which it was still attached near the bottom. While sitting under this tree both were instantly killed by lightning—"by touch etherial slain."

(**60.**) Jane⁵ Piper married Jacob Bradbury.

THEIR CHILDREN :

**109.** i. JOHN BRADBURY (*Jane⁵ Piper, Elisha⁴, Samuel³, Samuel², Nathaniel¹*), born March 22, 1805, in Limerick, Me.; a carpenter and teacher; married Mary Hill Burnham in March, 1829.

daughter of Esquire John and Mary (Hill) Burnham.  She was born
in 1804, in Limerick ; died Dec. 22, 1833. in Limerick, aged 29
years and 7 months.  He died Feb. 24, 1834, in Limerick, where
he resided.

**110.** ii.  BENJAMIN PIPER⁶ BRADBURY (*June⁵ Piper, Elisha⁴, Samuel³, Samuel², Nathaniel¹*), born June 6, 1807, in Limerick, Me.;
died Nov. 24, 1808, in Limerick.

**111.** iii.  JANE⁶ BRADBURY (*June⁵ Piper, Elisha⁴, Samuel³, Samuel², Nathaniel¹*), born Jan. 9, 1809, in Limerick, Me.; died June
2, 1885, in Limerick, where she resided.  The following obituary
notice of her appeared in one of the county papers :  " Her faith was
a positive one.  It never occurred to her to doubt the promises of
God.  As she lived so she died, trusting in her Redeemer."

**112.** iv.  ALBION⁶ BRADBURY (*June⁵ Piper, Elisha⁴, Samuel³,
Samuel², Nathaniel¹*) born May 6. 1810, in Limerick, Me.; a farmer ; married Elizabeth Liscomb Wentworth Jan. 10, 1856, daughter
of Shadrach and Lucy (Liscomb) Wentworth.  She was born June
13, 1831, in Acton, Me.  He died Nov. 21, 1882, in Limerick, on
the farm left him by his father.  He was a good farmer and respected citizen.*

**113.** v.  SALLY⁶ BRADBURY (*June⁵ Piper, Elisha⁴, Samuel³, Samuel², Nathaniel¹*), born March 31, 1815, in Limerick, Me., where
she now resides.  By her cheerful disposition she has added much to
the happiness of the family.

(**61.**) Betsey⁵ Piper married Isaac Felch.

THEIR CHILDREN :

**114.** i.  SUSAN⁶ FELCH (*Betsey⁵ Piper, Elisha⁴, Samuel³, Samuel², Nathaniel¹*), born Sept. 20, 1806, in Limerick, Me.; a teacher
before marriage ; married Thomas Carll Jan. 11, 1831, as his second wife, her cousin Jane Remick being his first.  He was born
in 1784, in Waterborough, Me.; a timber-dealer, lumber-manufacturer and representative in the Maine Legislature.  He died Oct.
17, 1865, at Salmon Falls, in Hollis, Me., where he then resided.
aged 81 years.  She died June 19, 1881, in Hollis.

**115.** ii.  NOAH⁵ FELCH (*Betsey⁵ Piper, Elisha⁴, Samuel³, Sam-

*Their children are as follows : 1. John Jacob, born Jan. 18, 1857.  2.
George Dana, born Dec. 6, 1858.  3. Annie Carlton, born Jan. 31, 1862.
4. Henry Sawtelle, born May 18, 1865 ; died July 25, 1867, in Limerick,
Me.  All were born in Limerick.

uel[2], Nathaniel[1]), born Sept. 25, 1808, in Limerick.  He resides in San Francisco, California.

**116.** iii. HANNAH RICKER[6] FELCH (Betsey[5] Piper, Elisha[4], Samuel[3], Samuel[2], Nathaniel[1]), born Feb. 19, 1810, in Limerick, Me.; a teacher before marriage ; married, as his second wife, Jonathan Stickney Evans April 28, 1845, born July 31, 1794, in Fryeburg, Me.; a farmer.  She died July 12, 1845, in Fryeburg.  He died March 24, 1857, in Fryeburg, where he always resided.

**117.** iv. ELIZA JANE[6] FELCH (Betsey[5] Piper, Elisha[4], Samuel[3], Samuel[2], Nathaniel[1]), born April 11, 1813, in Limerick, Me.; was educated at Parsonsfield Seminary, and a teacher before marriage ; married Elnathan Hunt Sept. 24, 1838, born July 7, 1804, in Gray, Me.; a farmer.  He resides in Gray.*

**118.** v. ISAAC NEWTON[6] FELCH (Betsey[5] Piper, Elisha[4], Samuel[3], Samuel[2], Nathaniel[1]), born Feb. 16, 1815, in Limerick, Me.; graduated at Bowdoin College in 1838 ; studied law, and was admitted to the bar in 1843 ; was editor of the " Progressive Age," " Waldo Signal" and the " Portland Evening Courier ;" and a member of the Maine Legislature for several years.  He married Isabella Nichols Johnson in Oct., 1841, born in 1818, in Brunswick, Me.; and died there July 2, 1873.  He died April 21, 1870, in Hollis, Me., where he then resided.  In a sketch of him which appeared in one of the Portland papers, the writer says : " He was popular in college, kindhearted and genial, ever thoroughly honest, and respected by all."†

**119.** vi. SARAH PIPER[6] FELCH (Betsey[5] Piper, Elisha[4], Samuel[3], Samuel[2], Nathaniel[1]), born March 10, 1818, in Parsonsfield, Me.; a teacher ; died April 23, 1841, in Gorham, Me., where she resided.

**120.** vii. LYDIA CLARK[6] FELCH (Betsey[5] Piper, Elisha[4], Samuel[3], Samuel[2], Nathaniel[1]), born Aug. 11, 1823, in Parsonsfield, Me.; a teacher, educated at Parsonsfield Seminary.  She was a young lady of much promise, and had bright prospects before her, but she did

*Their children are as follows : 1. Emma Weston, born Sept. 5, 1839. 2. Edwin Felch, born Feb. 4, 1841 ; died June 18, 1863, being a soldier in the Union Army. 3. Mary Elizabeth, born Oct. 27, 1842. 4. James Henry, born March 1, 1845. 5. George William, born Sept. 28, 1848. 6. Freeman Haskell, born July 2, 1851 ; died Aug. 11, 1854. 7. Jennie Carll, born June 22, 1854.  All were born in Gray, Me.

†Their children are : 1. Isabella, who died Aug. 16, 1861, aged 18 years. 2. William Johnson, Oct. 28, 1867, aged 22 years. 3. Lucretia Lawrence, June 6, 1861, aged 11 years.  They all died in Hollis, Me.

not live to enjoy them. She died Oct. 24, 1841, in Gorham, Me.,
at the early age of eighteen years.

(**62.**) Jonathan⁵ Piper married Mary Burbank.

THEIR CHILDREN :

**121.** i. HORACE⁶ PIPER (*Jonathan⁵*, *Elisha⁴*, *Samuel³*, *Samuel²*,
*Nathaniel¹*). born Dec. 30, 1810, in Parsonsfield, Me.; graduated
at Bowdoin College in 1838 ; received the degree of A. M. in 1841 ;
was Principal of Limerick Academy six years, from 1838 to 1844 ;
of Biddeford High School ten, from 1849 to 1859 ; and taught other
schools about four, in all about twenty years ; was trustee of Limerick Academy and Parsonsfield Seminary ; member, for York County, of the Board of Education of the State of Maine three years,
from 1846 to 1849 ; assisted Salem Town, LL. D., in preparing his
series of " Progressive Readers," and Benjamin Greenleaf, A. M.,
in revising his "Common School Arithmetic;" pursued a legal course
of study, and graduated at the Law School of the National University,
Washington, D. C., receiving the degree of LL. B. He married Josephine Bennett Lord, daughter of Richard and Lydia (Bennett)
Lord, Aug. 30, 1838, born July 16, 1816, in Parsonsfield, Me. She
was a woman of much decision of character, of a keen intellect, and a
kind and cheerful disposition. Her attachment to her family and
friends was strong, and her great desire was to make them happy.
She took a deep interest also in the welfare of others, and was
prompt and faithful in all her duties. In person she was a little
above the medium height, and of prepossessing appearance. She
united with the Second Congregational Church of Biddeford, Me.,
several years before her death, and lived a life consistent with her profession. She died Aug. 5, 1867, in Biddeford. He has resided in
Parsonsfield, Limerick, and Biddeford, and for the last twenty years
has lived in Washington, D.C.—SEE THEIR CHILDREN : Nos. **226,
227, 228.**

**122.** ii. IRVING⁶ PIPER ( *Jonathan⁵*, *Elisha⁴*, *Samuel³*, *Samuel²*,
*Nathaniel¹*). born Nov. 29, 1813, in Parsonsfield, Me. ; a farmer,
teacher, and town agent ; married, 1st, Mary Emery, daughter of
William and Lucy (Scammon) Emery, in 1841, born April 1, 1815, in
Buxton, Me., and died Feb. 6, 1847, in Parsonsfield ; 2d, Elizabeth
Chase, daughter of Edmund and Betsey (Day) Chase, Dec. 15, 1849,
born June 15, 1822, in Parsonsfield. She died Sept. 3, 1882, in
Poland, Me. Both of his wives were worthy women, and discharged

their household duties with ability. He died May 14, 1881, in Parsonsfield, on the homestead, devised to him by his father He was a good farmer, attentive to his business, and of high moral character.—SEE THEIR CHILD: No. 229.

**123.** iii. CATHARINE REDMAN⁶ PIPER (*Jonathan⁵, Elisha⁴, Samuel³, Samuel², Nathaniel¹*), born Dec. 23, 1815, in Parsonsfield Me. ; married Abram Fogg Marston, Oct. 3, 1847 : a farmer and selectman, born Oct. 5, 1819, in Effingham, N. H. Both he and his wife were members of the Freewill Baptist Church, and took a deep interest in the education of their children, and in all the benevolent movements for the improvement of society He died Dec. 4, 1887, on the old homestead where he resided, first purchased by his grandfather in the early settlement of the town.—SEE THEIR CHILDREN : Nos. 230, 231.

**124.** iv. OSBORNE BARKER⁶ PIPER (*Jonathan⁵, Elisha⁴, Samuel³, Samuel², Nathaniel¹*), born Jan. 25, 1819, in Parsonsfield, Me.; died May 20, 1873, in Parsonsfield, where he resided.                •

### SEVENTH GENERATION.

(**66.**) Saily⁶ Piper married Isaac Moore.

THEIR CHILDREN :

**125.** i. MARY JANE⁷ MOORE (*Sally⁶ Piper, Benjamin⁵, Elisha⁴, Samuel³, Samuel², Nathaniel¹*), born in Parsonsfield, Me.; a teacher before marriage ; married Caleb Burbank, the marriage certificate being granted Nov. 4, 1835. He was born March 31, 1804, in Parsonsfield ; a farmer and teacher. She died July 2, 1856, in Parsonsfield, aged 43 years and 7 months.* He died March 11, 1859, in Parsonsfield, where he always resided.

**126.** ii. CHARLES⁷ MOORE (*Sally⁶ Piper, Benjamin⁵, Elisha⁴, Samuel³, Samuel², Nathaniel¹*), born Nov. 10, 1816, in Parsonsfield, Me.; a sea-captain ; married Ann Carroll, June 21, 1841, born Nov. 15, 1816, in St. Johns, New Brunswick. He died Nov. 4, 1860, in Boston, Mass., and was buried in Mount Auburn Cemetery, Mass. His residence was in Boston.

**127.** iii. BENJAMIN PIPER⁷ MOORE (*Sally⁶ Piper, Benjamin⁵, Elisha⁴, Samuel³, Samuel², Nathaniel¹*), born in 1818, in Parsonsfield, Me.; a sea-captain ; married Ellen Carroll in 1851, born in

* This is her age and the time of her death given on her gravestone, but her brother Ira thinks she was a year younger. No record of her birth can now be found.

1819, in St. Johns, N. B.; died in 1876, in Boston, Mass.   He died
in 1874, in New York.   His residence was in Boston, Mass.

**128.** iv. CAROLINE⁷ MOORE (*Sally⁶ Piper, Benjamin⁵, Elisha⁴,
Samuel³, Samuel², Nathaniel¹*), born May 29, 1822, in Parsonsfield,
Me.; a teacher before marriage; married Amzi Libby Ayer, Sept.
14, 1848, born Oct. 22, 1824, in Limerick, Me.; a farmer.   She
died March 20, 1860, in Limerick.   He first resided in Limerick,
but subsequently removed to Biddeford, Me., where he now resides.

**129.** v. HARRIET ANN⁷ MOORE (*Sally⁶ Piper, Benjamin⁵, Elisha⁴,
Samuel³, Samuel², Nathaniel¹*), born in Parsonsfield, Me.; married
James Dearborn Wadleigh, Dec. 12, 1842, born Sept. 26, 1818, in
Parsonsfield ; a blacksmith.   She died July 8, 1853, in Gorham,
Me., aged 29 years and 9 months.   He died Dec. 22, 1872, in
Coaticook, Canada.   He resided in Gorham when his wife died,
but afterward removed to Coaticook.   She was buried in the ceme-
tery in North Parsonsfield, and he in Coaticook.

**130.** vi. ADDISON⁷ MOORE (*Sally⁶ Piper, Benjamin⁵, Elisha⁴,
Samuel³, Samuel², Nathaniel¹*), born about Nov. 7, 1827, in Parsonsfield, Me.; died June 7, 1828, in Parsonsfield, aged 7 months.

**131.** vii. IRA⁷ MORE* (*Sally⁶ Piper, Benjamin⁵, Elisha⁴, Samuel³, Samuel², Nathaniel¹*), born May 20, 1829, in Parsonsfield, Me.;
graduated at the State Normal School, at Bridgewater, Mass., in
1849, and afterward taught in the same school, and in Hingham,
Milton, and Newburyport, Mass.; graduated at the Scientific Department of Yale College in 1855 ; was elected first assistant in the
Chicago High School in 1856, and helped organize it, especially
the Normal Department ; in 1857 was elected to the Mathematical
Department of Illinois Normal University; in 1861 enlisted in the
33d Regiment of Illinois Infantry, and was made Captain of Company G ; served three years, and participated in the siege and capture of Vicksburg ; in 1864 resigned his commission as Captain on

---

* This name is spelled by some More, and by others Moore.   John and
Eben More, brothers, the former of whom settled in Parsonsfield in 1774,
and the latter, the same year, in Newfield near by, spelled their names
More.   The younger sons of John More changed their names to Moore,
and now nearly all the descendants of John and Eben spell their names
Moore.   Ira More has adhered to the spelling of his grandfather, John
More.   It is difficult to tell which is the original spelling.   Miss Hannah
More, the distinguished authoress, and Sir Thomas More, Lord Chancel-
lor of England, spelled their names More.   Thomas Moore, the poet, and
General Sir John Moore, the hero of Corunna, spelled theirs Moore.

account of ill health from hard service ; was Professor of Mathemat-
ics in the University of Minnesota in 1867 and 1869 ; in the latter
year was appointed Principal of Minnesota State Normal School ;
in 1875 removed to California, and taught in the State Normal
School at San José until 1883, since which time he has been Principal of the State Normal School at Los Angeles, Cal. He has
taught thirty-one full years, twenty-five of which were in normal
schools. He married Lucy Chesley Drew, daughter of Winborn A.
and Martha (Ayer) Drew, April 16, 1857. She was born Feb. 18,
1831, in Newfield, Me. ; graduated at Lapham Institute, at Crans-
ton, Rhode Island, and was a teacher in Limington Academy, Limington Me., and Limerick Academy, Limerick, Me., about three
years. He resides in Los Angeles, California.*

**132.** viii. ISAAC⁷ MOORE (*Sally⁶ Piper, Benjamin⁵. Elisha⁴,
Samuel³, Samuel², Nathaniel¹*), born about Oct. 17, 1833. in Parsonsfield, Me.; died May 17, 1836, in Parsonsfield, aged 2 years
and 7 months.

     (**67.**) Polly⁶ Piper married Gideon Bickford.

             THEIR CHILDREN :

**133.** i. HANNAH PIPER⁷ BICKFORD (*Polly⁶ Piper, Benjamin⁵,
Elisha⁴, Samuel³, Samuel², Nathaniel¹*), born July 9, 1818, in Par-
sonsfield, Me.; married George Washington Thompson, born in
Newfield, Me.; a factory overseer. She died Oct. 20, 1840, in
Parsonsfield ; he died. His residence was at Great Falls, N. H.,
at the time of his wife's death.

**134.** ii. MARY ANN⁷ BICKFORD (*Polly⁶ Piper, Benjamin⁵. Elisha⁴.
Samuel³, Samuel², Nathaniel¹*), born Aug. 20, 1820, in Parsonsfield,
Me.; married Andrew McChapman, June 6, 1841, born May 18,
1821, in Parsonsfield ; a farmer and merchant. He resides in Parsonsfield on the old homestead of his father on the North Road.

**135.** iii. HARRIET NEWELL⁷ BICKFORD (*Polly⁶ Piper, Benjamin⁵,
Elisha⁴, Samuel³, Samuel², Nathaniel¹*), born June 30, 1822, in
Parsonsfield, Me.; married Ivory G. March, May 5, 1847, born
May 8, 1820, in Parsonsfield ; a carpenter and farmer. He resides
in Monmouth, Me.

**136.** iv. GEORGE IRVING⁷ BICKFORD (*Polly⁶ Piper, Benjamin⁵,
Elisha⁴, Samuel³, Samuel², Nathaniel¹*), born Aug. 6, 1824, in

*Their children are as follows : 1. Kate, born Oct. 14, 1858, in Waukon,
Iowa. 2. Caroline, born April 5, 1861, in Normal, Ill.; died Jan. 28, 1878,
in San José, Cal. 3. Ira, born July 24, 1870, in St. Cloud, Minn.

Parsonsfield, Me.: a farmer; married Eliza Jane Parker May 10, 1845, born July 20, 1825, in Parsonsfield. He resides in Gorham, Me.

**137.** v. ALBION K. PARIS[7] BICKFORD (*Polly[6] Piper, Benjamin[5], Elisha[4], Samuel[3], Samuel[2], Nathaniel[1]*), born Oct. 24, 1826, in Parsonsfield, Me. ; a farmer; married Clarinda Jones March 28, 1852, born June 1, 1832, in Turner, Me. He resides in Turner.

**138.** vi. CYRUS[7] BICKFORD (*Polly[6] Piper, Benjamin[5], Elisha[4], Samuel[3], Samuel[2], Nathaniel[1]*), born July 12, 1829, in Parsonsfield, Me. ; died July 12, 1834, in Parsonsfield.

**139.** vii. ROSCOE GREENE[7] BICKFORD (*Polly[6] Piper, Benjamin[5], Elisha[4], Samuel[3], Samuel[2], Nathaniel[1]*), born Feb. 3, 1832, in Parsonsfield, Me. ; a farmer and carpenter; married Julia Ann Leavitt Jan. 1, 1856, born Jan. 15, 1837, in Parsonsfield. She died May 1, 1883, in Turner, Me. A short time ago he resided in Utica, Montana, but he now resides in Monmouth, Me.

**140.** viii. LAURINDA ELVIRA[7] BICKFORD (*Polly[6] Piper, Benjamin[5], Elisha[4], Samuel[3], Samuel[2], Nathaniel[1]*), born April 27, 1835, in Parsonsfield, Me.; married Almon Littlefield Feb. 27, 1874, born Jan. 10, 1841, in Standish, Me.; a farmer. He resides in Standish, near Sebago Lake.

**141.** ix. RUFUS MCINTIRE[7] BICKFORD (*Polly[6] Piper, Benjamin[5], Elisha[4], Samuel[3], Samuel[2], Nathaniel[1]*), born June 24, 1836, in Parsonsfield, Me.; a carpenter; married Martha Ann Kezar June 23, 1862, born May 2, 1844, in Parsonsfield. He resides in Romeo, Mich.

**142.** x. SARAH MOORE[7] BICKFORD (*Polly[6] Piper, Benjamin[5], Elisha[4], Samuel[3], Samuel[2], Nathaniel[1]*), born Aug. 2, 1838, in Parsonsfield, Me.; married Perry Rankin June 20, 1858, born May 28, 1834, in Hiram, Me.; a merchant. He resides in Waltham, Mass.

**143.** xi. ADALINE HANNAH[7] BICKFORD (*Polly[6] Piper, Benjamin[5], Elisha[4], Samuel[3], Samuel[2], Nathaniel[1]*), born May 19, 1842, in Parsonsfield, Me.; a teacher before marriage; married Simeon Strout Hobson May 26, 1861, born April 29, 1839, in Buxton, Me.; a farmer. She died Aug. 27, 1863, in Limington, Me. He resides in Utica, Montana.

(**68.**) Benjamin⁶ Piper married, 1st. Nancy
Sargent : 2d. Mercy Smith.

THEIR CHILDREN :

**144.** i. LORENZO DOW⁷ PIPER (*Benjamin⁶, Benjamin⁵, Elisha⁴.
Samuel³, Samuel², Nathaniel¹*), born Sept. 19, 1829. in Parsonsfield. Me.: a farmer. teacher. and high sheriff of Mitchell County,
Iowa ; married Mary Jane Nason Sept 26. 1850. born March 27,
1829, in South Berwick. Me.  The "History of Mitchell County"
says of him : " In 1857 he came to Iowa.  In 1873 he was
elected high sheriff of Mitchell County. which office he held three
terms.  After his term of office expired he returned to his farm and
engaged in farming. which occupation he still follows.  He has
built one of the finest farm-houses in the county. at a cost of three
thousand five hundred dollars, and a barn costing one thousand two
hundred.  Mr. Piper and family are members of the Congregational
Church."  He resides in West Mitchell, Iowa.—SEE THEIR CHIL-
DREN : Nos. **232. 233.**

**145.** ii. JOSEPH PERKINS⁷ PIPER (*Benjamin⁶, Benjamin⁵. Elisha⁴.
Samuel³. Samuel². Nathaniel¹*), born July 9. 1831, in Shapleigh. Me.;
is in railroad-business ; married Ann Maria Frost Sept. 23. 1852.
born Sept. 23. 1836. in Parsonsfield. Me.  He resides in Charlestown, Mass.—SEE THEIR CHILDREN : Nos. **234. 235.**

**146.** iii. CHARLES ABBOTT⁷ PIPER (*Benjamin⁶, Benjamin⁵, Elisha⁴,. Samuel³, Samuel², Nathaniel¹*), born Jan. 18, 1835. in
Shapleigh. Me.; a painter and photographer ; married Mary Emeline Hall July 9. 1854. born June 15. 1832. in Shapleigh.  She
died Dec. 21, 1878. in Biddeford. Me.  He resides in Charlestown,
Mass.—SEE THEIR CHILDREN : Nos. **236. 237. 238. 239. 240.
241.**

**147.** iv. SARAH JANE⁷ PIPER (*Benjamin⁶, Benjamin⁵, Elisha⁴.
Samuel³. Samuel². Nathaniel¹*). born January. 1838, in Shapleigh,
Me.; died July 24. 1841, in Shapleigh.

**148.** v. HORACE MANSON⁷ PIPER (*Benjamin⁶. Benjamin⁵, Elisha⁴,
Samuel³, Samuel². Nathaniel¹*). born May 11. 1844. in Parsonsfield,
Me.; a carpenter. teacher. and soldier in the Union Army in the
War of the Rebellion, in the 27th Iowa Infantry, Co. K : fought
in the battles of Lake Chico, Pleasant Hill, Tupelo, Oldtown Creek,
and Nashville.  He married. 1st. Hannah Wedgwood Moore April
9. 1872, born Dec. 2. 1844. in Newfield. Me.: died May 30. 1879.

in Newfield ; 2d. Emma Mary Joy Dec. 20, 1881, born Oct. 22, 1861, in Mitchell, Iowa. He resides in Minneapolis, Minn. They have no children.

(**69.**) Lavinia⁶ Piper married Hiram Harding.

THEIR CHILDREN :

**149.** i. LODNOK⁷ HARDING (*Lavinia⁶ Piper, David⁵, Elisha⁴, Samuel³, Samuel², Nathaniel¹*), born Dec. 8, 1815, in Hampden, Me.; a car upholsterer ; married Mary Gray Feb. 19, 1839, born Aug. 1, 1816, in Clermont County, Ohio. He resides in Ludlow, Ky.*

**150.** ii. SUSAN⁷ HARDING (*Lavinia⁶ Piper, David⁵, Elisha⁴, Samuel³, Samuel², Nathaniel¹*), born Apr. 12, 1817, in Hampden, Me.; married Marcus Pumpelly, born in Turner, Me.; a cooper. She died March 25, 1842, in Amelia, Ohio, where they resided.

**151.** iii. LAVINIA⁷ HARDING (*Lavinia⁶ Piper, David⁵, Elisha⁴, Samuel³, Samuel², Nathaniel¹*), born Jan. 1, 1819, in New Richmond, Ohio ; married David E. White Sept. 28, 1834, born in Batavia, Ohio. He resides in Bloomington, Ill.

**152.** iv. HIRAM⁷ HARDING (*Lavinia⁶ Piper, David⁵, Elisha⁴, Samuel³, Samuel², Nathaniel¹*), born Sept. 8, 1821, in New Richmond, Ohio ; died Aug. 21, 1829, in New Richmond.

**153.** v. JULIA ANN⁷ HARDING (*Lavinia⁶ Piper, David⁵, Elisha⁴, Samuel³, Samuel², Nathaniel¹*), born July 27, 1827, in New Richmond, Ohio ; married Rufus P. White ; a painter, born in Ohio. She died Apr. 24, 1848, in Amelia, Ohio, where they then resided. He now resides in Cincinnati, Ohio.

(**70.**) Ezekiel⁶ Piper married Ann Roberts.

THEIR CHILDREN.

**154.** i. PERRY H.⁷ PIPER (*Ezekiel⁶, David⁵, Elisha⁴, Samuel³, Samuel², Nathaniel¹*), born Aug. 8, 1819, in Harveysburg, Ohio. He went to Illinois in 1836 ; married Harriet Hart Savage Aug. 31, 1843, born Jan. 11, 1827, in Jacksonville, Ill. He pursued the business of farming till 1876, when he sold his farm and removed into the city of Princeton, Ill., and invested his money in bank

---

* Their children are as follows : 1. Valeria, born Jan. 3, 1840, in Batavia, Ohio. 2. Albert, born Feb. 12, 1842, in Perin, Ohio. 3. Susan, born Feb. 7, 1844, in Perin, Ohio. 4. Olive, born Dec. 4, 1857, in Perin, Ohio. 5. Edgar H., born Sept. 18, 1859, in Cochran, Ind.

stock. He is now engaged in real estate business, and is director
of a bank. He resides in Princeton.—SEE THEIR CHILDREN : Nos.
**242, 243, 244, 245.**

**155.** ii. DAVID⁷ PIPER (*Ezekiel⁶, David⁵, Elisha⁴, Samuel³, Samuel², Nathaniel¹*), born Oct. 17, 1822, in Harveysburg, Ohio ; a
farmer ; married Philipina Heintz Aug. 31, 1848, born Sept. 16,
1816, at Edenkoben, in Bavaria, Germany. He died Dec. 26,
1867, in Ottville, Ill., being killed by the accidental discharge of a
gun while on a hunting excursion. He resided in Hollowayville,
Ill.—SEE THEIR CHILDREN : Nos. **246, 247, 248, 249, 250.**

**156.** iii. MARINDA⁷ PIPER (*Ezekiel⁶, David⁵, Elisha⁴, Samuel³,
Samuel², Nathaniel¹*), born Jan. 30, 1825, in Harveysburg, Ohio ;
married Frederick Heintz Feb. 8, 1844, born May 4, 1814, in Germany ; a farmer. He resides in Hollowayville, Ill.—SEE THEIR
CHILDREN : Nos. **251, 252, 253, 254.**

**157.** iv. HIRAM HARDING⁷ PIPER (*Ezekiel⁶, David⁵, Elisha⁴, Samuel³, Samuel², Nathaniel¹*), born Dec. 11, 1828, in Harveysburg.
Ohio ; a farmer ; married Mary Amanda McWilliams, daughter of
William T. and Mary Ann McWilliams, Dec. 18, 1859. born Jan. 16,
1841, in Middletown, Ohio. She died Nov. 9, 1876, in Malden,
Ill. He is a large land-holder, and carries on farming extensively,
owning two thousand and sixty-five acres of land. His farm at
home, which he cultivates, contains three hundred and twenty acres
of this, and the remainder is rented to tenants. It is located in
different townships, some in Berlin, and some in Hall and Selby.
The land being valuable affords a large income from the rents, and is
constantly increasing in value. He has rendered me important
assistance in collecting genealogies for this book. See page 8. He
resides in Malden, Ill.—SEE THEIR CHILDREN : Nos. **255, 256,
257, 258, 259, 260, 261, 262, 263, 264.**

**158.** v. MARY ANN⁷ PIPER (*Ezekiel⁶, David⁵, Elisha⁴, Samuel³,
Samuel², Nathaniel¹*), born Sept. 3, 1830, in Harveysburg, Ohio ;
married William Simon Dalton Jan. 1, 1855, born Dec. 2, 1824,
in Mason, Ohio ; a farmer. He died July 16, 1887, in Malden,
Ill., where he resided.—SEE THEIR CHILDREN, Nos. **265, 266,
267, 268, 269, 270, 271.**

**159.** vi. LAVINIA HARDING⁷ PIPER (*Ezekiel⁶, David⁵, Elisha⁴,
Samuel³, Samuel², Nathaniel¹*), born Jan. 20, 1833, in Princeton,
Ill.; married Jonathan Oglesbee Feb. 24, 1858, born Sept. 30,

1830, in Harveysburg, Ohio ; a farmer. She died Oct. 6, 1864, in Harveysburg. He resides in Harveysburg,--SEE THEIR CHILDREN : Nos. **272, 273, 274.**

**160.** vii. WILLIAM WILKINSON⁷ PIPER (*Ezekiel⁶, David⁵, Elisha⁴, Samuel³, Samuel², Nathaniel¹*), born Feb. 20, 1836, in Harveysburg, Ohio ; a farmer ; married, 1st, Lydia Ann Savage March 12, 1856, born Oct. 6, 1840, in Selby, Ill.; died Nov. 1, 1868, in Selby ; 2d, Cordelia Barrett (maiden name Cordelia Young) March 7, 1869, born June 17, 1842, in Addison, N. Y. He resides in Princeton, Ill.—SEE THEIR CHILDREN : Nos. **275, 276, 277.** .

(74.) Elisha⁶ Piper married Ann Lewis.

THEIR CHILDREN :

**161.** i. DAVID CLINTON⁷ PIPER (*Elisha⁶, David⁵, Elisha⁴, Samuel³, Samuel², Nathaniel¹*), born June 14, 1826, in Cincinnati, Ohio ; a farmer. He resides in Selby, Ill., and is the only one of the family living.

**162.** ii. GEORGE LEWIS⁷ PIPER (*Elisha⁶, David⁵, Elisha⁴, Samuel³, Samuel², Nathaniel¹*), born March 24, 1829, in Cincinnati, Ohio; a farmer ; married Nancy Long Feb. 26, 1854, born April 20, 1834, in Xenia, Ohio. He died Feb. 13, 1870, in Selby, Ill. They had no children.

**163.** iii. MARY ANN⁷ PIPER (*Elisha⁶, David⁵, Elisha⁴, Samuel³, Samuel², Nathaniel¹*), born March 12, 1831, near Cincinnati, Ohio ; married John Guilford Combs Dec. 13, 1848, born April 19, 1821, in Grainger County, Tenn.; a farmer. She died Nov. 26, 1868, in Hall, Ill., where they then resided. He now resides in Auburn, Neb.--SEE THEIR CHILDREN : Nos. **278, 279, 280, 281, 282.**

**164.** iv. WILLIAM HARDING⁷ PIPER (*Elisha⁶, David⁵, Elisha⁴, Samuel³, Samuel², Nathaniel¹*), born Sept. 8, 1837, near Cincinnati, Ohio ; a farmer ; died Dec. 13, 1863, at Holly Springs, Miss. His residence was in Selby, Ill.

**165.** v. JOHN COXTON⁷ PIPER (*Elisha⁶, David⁵, Elisha⁴, Samuel³, Samuel², Nathaniel¹*), born Feb. 26, 1839, in Leepertown, Ill.; a farmer ; died April 26, 1864, in Selby, Ill., where he resided.

**166.** vi. CAROLINE⁷ PIPER (*Elisha⁶, David⁵, Elisha⁴, Samuel³, Samuel², Nathaniel¹*), born Jan. 16, 1833, near Cincinnati, Ohio ; married Francis Marion Long March 20, 1852, born Jan. 11, 1832, in Xenia, Ohio ; a farmer. She died Dec. 16, 1862, in Selby, Ill.,

where they then resided.   He now resides in Vinton, Iowa.—SEE
THEIR CHILDREN :  Nos. **283, 284, 285, 286.**

**167.** vii. EZEKIEL⁷ PIPER (*Elisha⁶, David⁵, Elisha⁴, Samuel³,
Samuel², Nathaniel¹*), born Oct. 20, 1835, near Cincinnati, Ohio ;
a farmer.   He died May 16, 1865, in Selby, Ill., where he resided.

(**72.**) Nancy Frothingham⁶ Piper married David Jemegan.

THEIR CHILDREN :

**168.** i. MARY THAXTER⁷ JEMEGAN (*Nancy Frothingham⁶ Piper,
David⁵, Elisha⁴, Samuel³, Samuel², Nathaniel¹*), born Apr. 15, 1832,
in Amelia, Ohio ; married William Crossman McGill, Oct. 7, 1850,
born Aug. 24, 1824, in Lowellville, Ohio ; a teacher.   She has
rendered me valuable assistance in collecting genealogies for this
book.   See page 9.   They reside in Amelia.*

**169.** ii. HULDAH ANN⁷ JEMEGAN (*Nancy Frothingham⁶ Piper,
David⁵, Elisha⁴, Samuel³, Samuel², Nathaniel¹*), born Nov. 21, 1833,
in Amelia, Ohio ; married Hope Brown Miller, Aug. 23, 1855, born
June 23, 1832, at Flagg Spring, Ky.; a merchant.   She died Feb.
15, 1856, at Mount Washington, Ohio, where they then resided.
He now resides in Michigan City, Ind.

(**79.**) Thomas Parsons⁶ Piper married, 1st, Lucy Turner
Gilmore ; 2d, Abigail Burdick True.

THEIR CHILDREN :

**170.** i. ALBERT PARSONS⁷ PIPER (*Thomas Parsons⁶, Daniel⁵,
Elisha⁴, Samuel³, Samuel², Nathaniel¹*), born Jan. 20, 1830, in
Newburgh, Me.; a carriage-maker ; married, 1st, Abby Richards
Towle, May 11, 1853, born June 2, 1833, in Searsport, Me.; died
April 22, 1870, in Belfast, Me.; 2d, Maria Arnold Vose, Dec. 24,
1872, born March 25, 1842, in Warren, Me.   He resides in Thom-
aston, Me.—SEE THEIR CHILDREN : Nos. **287, 288.**

**171.** ii. MARILLA MARKS⁷ PIPER (*Thomas Parsons⁶, Daniel⁵,
Elisha⁴, Samuel³, Samuel², Nathaniel¹*), born Aug. 1, 1833, in
Newburgh, Me.; a teacher before marriage ; married John Bradford
Mason, Aug. 29, 1852, born Aug. 12, 1830, in Searsport, Me.; a
master mariner.   His residence is in Jacksonville, Florida.   They
have no children.

* Their children are as follows : 1. Mary Fredonia, born June 21, 1854,
in Germantown, Ky.; died Sept. 24, 1854, in Amelia, Ohio.   2. Huldah
Lunetta, born Jan. 1, 1856, in Greensburg, Ind.; died March 12, 1861, in
Amelia   3. William Jemegan, born March 24, 1862, in Amelia.   4. Nan-
nie Ray, born Jan. 7, 1871, in Amelia.

**172.** iii. CHARLES RIGBY[7] PIPER (*Thomas Parsons⁶, Daniel⁵, Elisha⁴, Samuel³, Samuel², Nathaniel¹*), born Aug. 11, 1841, in Newburgh, Me.; died Feb. 15, 1843, in Newburgh.

(**81.**) Benjamin⁶ Piper married Julia Bickford.

THEIR CHILDREN :

**173.** i. CHARLES PARSONS[7] PIPER (*Benjamin⁶, Daniel⁵, Elisha⁴, Samuel³, Samuel², Nathaniel¹*), born Aug. 29, 1830, in Newburgh, Me.; died Aug. 19, 1833, in Newburgh.

**174.** ii. SUSAN BICKFORD[7] PIPER (*Benjamin⁶, Daniel⁵, Elisha⁴, Samuel³, Samuel², Nathaniel¹*), born Dec. 8, 1832, in Newburgh, Me.; married Byron Porter, March 22, 1852, born Nov. 20, 1829, in Dixmont, Me.; a farmer, teacher, and merchant. She died April 5, 1871, in Bangor, Me., where they then resided. He now resides in Upper Stillwater, Me.—SEE THEIR CHILD : No. **289.**

**175.** iii. DANIEL[7] PIPER (*Benjamin⁶, Daniel⁵, Elisha⁴, Samuel³, Samuel², Nathaniel¹*), born Feb. 8, 1834, in Newburgh, Me.; a merchant ; married Helen Wildes, Dec. 2, 1855, born March 30, 1830, in Monroe, Me. He died Aug. 25, 1874, in Dixmont, Me., where he resided.—SEE THEIR CHILDREN : Nos. **290, 291, 292, 293.**

**176.** iv. JULIA ANN[7] PIPER (*Benjamin⁶, Daniel⁵, Elisha⁴, Samuel³, Samuel², Nathaniel¹*), born July 19, 1840, in Newburgh, Me.; married Edwin Harris, Sept. 28, 1870, born March 17, 1846, in Clinton, Mass.; a merchant. He resides in Boston, Mass. They have no children.

**177.** v. WARREN LINCOLN[7] PIPER (*Benjamin⁶, Daniel⁵, Elisha⁴, Samuel³, Samuel², Nathaniel¹*), born Dec. 6, 1841, in Newburgh, Me.; a farmer and soldier in the Union Army in the War of the Rebellion, Co. K, 1st Maine Heavy Artillery ; died of small-pox April 2, 1864, in the hospital at Georgetown, D. C. He resided in Monroe, Me.

**178.** vi. EVELYN NEWCOMB[7] PIPER (*Benjamin⁶, Daniel⁵, Elisha⁴, Samuel³, Samuel², Nathaniel¹*), born Jan. 2, 1844, in Newburgh, Me.; a teacher before marriage ; married George Harvey Rutledge, April 11, 1884, born Aug. 3, 1842, in Springfield, Mass.; a merchant. I am indebted to her for furnishing me the genealogies of several of the Piper families. He resides in Boston, Mass. They have no children.

**179.** vii. BENJAMIN[7] PIPER (*Benjamin⁶, Daniel⁵, Elisha⁴, Samuel³, Samuel², Nathaniel¹*), born Jan. 14, 1851, in Dixmont, Me.;

a farmer and postmaster; married Ora Johnson, March 4, 1876, born Feb. 3, 1856, in Dixmont, Me. He died Feb. 3, 1877, in Dixmont, where he always resided. They had no children.

(**82.**) Elisha⁵ Piper married Rhoda Hilton Bickford.

### THEIR CHILDREN :

**180.** i. ELISHA SANFORN⁷ PIPER (*Elisha⁶, Daniel⁵, Elisha⁴, Samuel³, Samuel², Nathaniel¹*), born Dec. 21, 1835, in Newburgh, Me.; a policeman; married Eliza Jane Smith, June 4, 1856, born Sept. 21, 1836, in Monroe, Me. He resides in Medford, Mass.—SEE THEIR CHILDREN : Nos. **291, 295, 296, 297, 298.**

**181.** ii. ENOCH FRANKLIN⁷ PIPER (*Elisha⁶, Daniel⁵, Elisha⁴, Samuel³, Samuel², Nathaniel¹*), born June 28, 1838, in Newburgh, Me.; a farmer; married Adella Whitcomb, July 4, 1860, born Oct. 11, 1842, in Augusta, Me. He resides in Dixmont, Me.—SEE THEIR CHILDREN : Nos. **299, 300, 301, 302.**

**182.** iii. EUNICE FRANCES⁷ PIPER (*Elisha⁶, Daniel⁵, Elisha⁴, Samuel³, Samuel², Nathaniel¹*), born June 28, 1838, in Newburgh, Me., died Dec. 31, 1839, in Newburgh. Eunice Frances⁷ and Enoch Franklin⁷ were twins.

**183.** iv. RHODA ADDIE⁷ PIPER (*Elisha⁶, Daniel⁵, Elisha⁴, Samuel³, Samuel², Nathaniel¹*), born Jan. 10, 1849, in Newburgh, Me.; married William Henry Hollis, Jan. 11, 1865, born Nov. 5, 1840, in Troy, Me.; a farmer. They reside in Newburgh.—SEE THEIR CHILDREN : Nos. **363, 364.**

**184.** v. SUSAN EMMA⁷ PIPER (*Elisha⁶, Daniel⁵, Elisha⁴, Samuel³, Samuel², Nathaniel¹*), born Jan. 10, 1849, in Newburgh, Me.; married Samuel Woodman Bridgham, Dec. 17, 1865, born Sept. 10, 1837, in Bangor, Me.; a mill-man. Susan Emma⁷ and Rhoda Addie⁷ are twins. He resides in Newburgh.—SEE THEIR CHILDREN : Nos. **305, 306, 307.**

(**83.**) Hannah Foster⁶ Piper married Elijah Bachelder.

### THEIR CHILDREN :

**185.** i. MELVIN⁷ BACHELDER (*Hannah Foster⁶ Piper, Daniel⁵, Elisha⁴, Samuel³, Samuel², Nathaniel¹*), born Oct. 23, 1835, in Prospect, Me.; a farmer; married Jennie Connor Libby, Dec. 30, 1869, born Sept. 26, 1848, in Troy, Me. They reside in Fairfield, Me.*

* They have one child, Adella, born Dec. 21, 1873, in Dixmont, Me.

**186.** ii. JAMES MARDEN⁷ BACHELDER (*Hannah Foster⁶ Piper, Daniel⁵, Elisha⁴, Samuel³, Samuel², Nathaniel¹*), born Feb. 28, 1837, in Prospect, Me.; died March 7, 1838, in Prospect.

**187.** iii. KINGSBURY⁷ BACHELDER (*Hannah Foster⁶ Piper, Daniel⁵, Elisha⁴, Samuel³, Samuel², Nathaniel¹*), born Oct. 27, 1841, in Prospect, Me.; graduated from Bowdoin College in 1871. While in college he obtained a prize of thirty dollars for the best examination in Latin, at the end of the sophomore year. In his senior year he won a prize of ten dollars for the best oration, and on graduating, the Latin salutatory oration was assigned to him. He taught Auburn High School at Auburn, Me., one year, and was Principal of the Maine Central Institute at Pittsfield, Me., eight years. He pursued a theological course of study in the Theological School of Bates College. On resigning his position as Principal of the Maine Central Institute in 1883, he was elected Waldron Professor of the Latin language and literature in Hillsdale College at Hillsdale, Michigan, and in 1887 was made Professor of the Greek language and literature. He is also a Trustee of the college and one of the Directors of the "Morning Star," a Freewill Baptist paper published in Boston, Mass. He has been Professor in Hillsdale College five years, and the whole time during which he has been engaged as teacher and professor exceeds fourteen full years. He married Mary Augusta Wade, June 27, 1877, daughter of Ebenezer Delano and Mary Ripley (Dyer) Wade. She was born Jan. 29, 1851, in Parkman, Me.; graduated in 1870 at the Maine State Seminary, at Lewiston, Me., and after graduation taught several terms in Fryeburg Academy. They reside in Hillsdale, Mich. They have no children.

**188.** iv. CATHERINE PIPER⁷ BACHELDER (*Hannah Foster⁶ Piper, Daniel⁵, Elisha⁴, Samuel³, Samuel², Nathaniel¹*), born Jan. 11, 1844, in Newburgh, Me.; married Ephraim Dodge Bartlett, Aug. 30, 1862, born Feb. 15, 1841, in Newburgh. He resides in Newburgh.*

---

* Their children are as follows : 1. Annie Cora, born May 5, 1864. 2. Martha Jane, born May 3, 1866. 3. Lydia Etta, born Dec. 22, 1868. 4. Daisy Belle, born Dec. 20, 1870. 5. Emma Ethel, born Oct. 7, 1873. 6. Percy Ludelle, born Jan. 30, 1881. They were all born in Newburgh, Me.

**(86.)** Daniel⁶ Piper married Hannah Foster Parsons.

THEIR CHILD:

**189.** I. ELIZA ANN⁷ PIPER (*Daniel⁶*, *Daniel⁵*, *Elisha⁴*, *Samuel³*, *Samuel²*, *Nathaniel¹*), born Aug. 19, 1850, in Parsonsfield, Me.; married Brackett Tobias Lord, Jan. 13, 1870, born July 29, 1847, in Cornish, Me.; a farmer and selectman. He resides on the Middle Road, in Parsonsfield.—SEE THEIR CHILDREN : Nos. **308, 309.**

**(87.)** Simeon Barker⁶ Piper married, 1st. Hannah
Kaylor ; 2d, Harriet Augusta Wildes.

THEIR CHILDREN :

**190.** i. FREDERICK AUGUSTUS⁷ PIPER (*Simeon Barker⁶*, *Daniel⁵*, *Elisha⁴*, *Samuel³*, *Samuel²*, *Nathaniel¹*), born Sept. 5, 1843, in Jefferson Barracks, Mo.; a lawyer and special examiner of pension claims in the United States Pension Office. He graduated at the Law School of the National University, Washington, D. C., and received the degree of LL.B. He was also a soldier in the Union Army in the War of the Rebellion, was several times under fire of the enemy, and was wounded in the battle of the Wilderness. He married Aurora Low, Oct. 26, 1870, born Aug. 28, 1847, in Frankfort, Me. His residence is in Monroe, Me.—SEE THEIR CHILD : No. **310.**

**191.** ii. ANNA⁷ PIPER (*Simeon Barker⁶*, *Daniel⁵*, *Elisha⁴*, *Samuel³*, *Samuel²*, *Nathaniel¹*), born Aug. 4, 1844, in New Orleans, La. She resides in Belfast, Me.

**192.** iii. SIMEON BARKER⁷ PIPER (*Simeon Barker⁶*, *Daniel⁵*, *Elisha⁴*, *Samuel³*, *Samuel²*, *Nathaniel¹*), born Dec. 12, 1846, in New Orleans, La.; a photographer and soldier in the 1st Maine Heavy Artillery in the Union Army, in the War of the Rebellion ; married Maria Elizabeth Wheeler, Jan. 27, 1873, born July 13, 1853, in Elizabeth, N. J. He resides in York, Pa.—SEE THEIR CHILDREN : Nos. **311, 312, 313.**

**193.** iv. HELEN AUGUSTA⁷ PIPER (*Simeon Barker⁶*, *Daniel⁵*, *Elisha⁴*, *Samuel³*, *Samuel²*, *Nathaniel¹*) born May 29, 1858, in Monroe, Me.; married Peter Cooper, son of Cornelius and Lavinia (Cubberly) Cooper, born Sept. 11, 1847, in Somerville, N. J.; a printer. He resides in Elizabeth, N. J.—SEE THEIR CHILDREN : Nos. **314, 315.**

**(88.)** Alpheus Felch[6] Piper married, 1st, Catharine Smart Perkins; 2d, Susan Hannah Smith.

**191.** i. DAVID MANSER[7] PIPER (*Alpheus Felch[6], Daniel[5], Elisha[4], Samuel[3], Samuel[2], Nathaniel[1]*), born May 20, 1854, in Monroe, Me.; a farmer; married Lizzie Rushton. June 15, 1881, born in Maine. He resides in Swanville, Me. They have no children.

**195.** ii. WYMAN BROWN[7] PIPER (*Alpheus Felch[6], Daniel[5], Elisha[4], Samuel[3], Samuel[2], Nathaniel[1]*), born Dec. 14, 1855, in Monroe, Me.; a teacher. He commenced teaching in 1871, at the age of fifteen, and has taught every year since. He graduated at the Maine Central Institute, and afterward entered Bates College, where he remained for some time. He was Principal of Corinna Union Academy for four years, till 1882, and has recently been elected Principal of Lodi High School, at Lodi, Cal. While at Corinna he was a member of the superintending school committee three years, and Captain of Corinna Light Infantry. He married Annie Cole Russell, daughter of Eli and Hannah (Spofford) Russell, Feb. 25, 1877. She was born Aug. 20, 1855, in Monticello, Me. He resides in Lodi, Cal.—SEE THEIR CHILDREN : Nos. **316, 317.**

**196.** iii. LIZZIE MAY[7] PIPER (*Alpheus Felch[6], Daniel[5], Elisha[4], Samuel[3], Samuel[2], Nathaniel[1]*), born Oct. 11, 1857, in Monroe, Me.; married Joseph Granville Patterson, Oct. 28, 1878, born Apr. 10, 1854, in Swanville, Me.; a ship-joiner. He resides in Belfast, Me.—SEE THEIR CHILD : No. **318.**

**197.** iv. KINGSBURY BACHELDER[7] PIPER (*Alpheus Felch[6], Daniel[5], Elisha[4], Samuel[3], Samuel[2], Nathaniel[1]*), born Feb. 4, 1866, in Monroe, Me.; a teacher. He has taught in several towns in Maine, and in Freeport and Clemens, Cal., about three years. He married Inez Victoria Morse, daughter of Joseph Horace and Eliza Jane (Garland) Morse, May 2, 1889, born Jan. 30, 1866, in Dixmont, Me. She was a teacher before marriage, and has taught five years in Dixmont and other towns in Maine, being employed a part of the time as a teacher in High Schools. He resides in Waterville, Me. They have no children.

**198.** v. LURILLA MASON[7] PIPER (*Alpheus Felch[6], Daniel[5], Elisha[4], Samuel[3], Samuel[2], Nathaniel[1]*), born Feb. 19, 1867, in Monroe, Me.; a teacher before marriage for several years; married Oscar Harvey

Fall, March 4, 1885, born Sept. 3, 1858, in Newburgh, Me.; a farmer, school supervisor, and master of the Golden Rule Grange. He resides in Newburgh. They have no children.

(**89.**) John Usher Parsons[6] Piper married Elizabeth Packard.

THEIR CHILDREN:

**199.** i. LUCY ANN[7] PIPER (*John Usher Parsons[6], Daniel[5], Elisha[4], Samuel[3], Samuel[2], Nathaniel[1]*), born May 3, 1846, in Newburgh, Me.; died Sept. 19, 1850, in Newburgh.

**200.** ii. ELISHA FRANKLIN[7] PIPER (*John Usher Parsons[6], Daniel[5], Elisha[4], Samuel[3], Samuel[2], Nathaniel[1]*), born June 15, 1848, in Newburgh, Me.; a merchant; married, 1st, Edith Snow, Oct. 19, 1871, born Nov. 23, 1853, in Newburgh; died June 1st, 1881, in Newburgh; 2d, Sabra Reed, June 15, 1884, born Nov. 18, 1856, in Bangor, Me. He resides in Bangor.—SEE THEIR CHILDREN: Nos. **319, 320, 321, 322.**

**201.** iii. JOHN USHER PARSONS[7] PIPER (*John Usher Parsons[6], Daniel[5], Elisha[4], Samuel[3], Samuel[2], Nathaniel[1]*), born July 4, 1861, in Winterport, Me.; died Aug. 8, 1862, in Winterport.

(**102.**) Sally[6] Piper married Gideon Leavitt.

THEIR CHILDREN:

**202.** i. NANCY MIGHELS[7] LEAVITT (*Sally[6] Piper, Elisha[5], Elisha[4], Samuel[3], Samuel[2], Nathaniel[1]*), born Oct. 13, 1825, in Newburgh, Me.; died Aug. 29, 1826, in Newburgh.

**203.** ii. SALLY ANN[7] LEAVITT (*Sally[6] Piper, Elisha[5], Elisha[4], Samuel[3], Samuel[2], Nathaniel[1]*), born Feb. 9, 1827, in Newburgh, Me.; married Robert Billings Thomas, Jan. 12, 1855, born July 14, 1823, in Newburgh; a farmer. He resides in Newburgh.

**204.** iii. JESSE JAMES[7] LEAVITT (*Sally[6] Piper, Elisha[5], Elisha[4], Samuel[3], Samuel[2], Nathaniel[1]*), born Sept. 15, 1828, in Newburgh, Me.; died Jan. 6, 1841, in Newburgh.

**205.** iv. ELISHA FRANKLIN[7] LEAVITT (*Sally[6] Piper, Elisha[5], Elisha[4], Samuel[3], Samuel[2], Nathaniel[1]*), born Dec. 1, 1829, in Newburgh, Me.; died Jan. 1, 1841, in Newburgh.

**206.** v. HARRIET[7] LEAVITT (*Sally[6] Piper, Elisha[5], Elisha[4], Samuel[3], Samuel[2], Nathaniel[1]*), born Aug. 8, 1831, in Newburgh, Me.; died Sept. 20, 1832, in Newburgh.

**207.** vi. DAVID PIPER[7] LEAVITT (*Sally[6] Piper, Elisha[5], Elisha[4], Samuel[3], Samuel[2], Nathaniel[1]*), born June 16, 1833, in Newburgh, Me.; a farmer; died July 25, 1856, in Bangor, Me.

**208.** vii. WILLIAM BURKE[7] LEAVITT (*Sally[6] Piper, Elisha[5], Elisha[4], Samuel[3], Samuel[2], Nathaniel[1]*). born March 22, 1835, in Newburgh, Me.; a miner. He resides in Colorado.

**209.** viii. JUDITH[7] LEAVITT (*Sally[6] Piper, Elisha[5], Elisha[4], Samuel[3], Samuel[2], Nathaniel[1]*), born Feb. 16, 1837, in Newburgh, . Me.; died June 2, 1840, in Newburgh.

**210.** ix. JOHN BRADBURY[7] LEAVITT (*Sally[6] Piper, Elisha[5], Elisha[4], Samuel[3], Samuel[2], Nathaniel[1]*), born Feb. 16, 1839, in Newburgh, Me.; a farmer; married Marietta Chase, Sept. 25, 1857, born May 25, 1841, in Bangor, Me. He resides in Newburgh.

**211.** x. ELISHA FRANKLIN[7] LEAVITT (*Sally[6] Piper, Elisha[5], Elisha[4], Samuel[3], Samuel[2], Nathaniel[1]*), born Nov. 10, 1840*, in Newburgh, Me.; a farmer; died June 14, 1862, in Newburgh, where he resided.

**212.** xi. ELMA FRANCES[7] LEAVITT (*Sally[6] Piper, Elisha[5], Elisha[4], Samuel[3], Samuel[2], Nathaniel[1]*), born Jan. 19, 1843, in Newburgh, Me.; a teacher; married Greenfield Gardner Bickford, Oct. 21, 1868, born May 18, 1841, in Newburgh; a farmer. She died April 21, 1872, in Newburgh. He resided in Newburgh when his wife died, but now resides in Monroe, Me.

(**103.**) Betsey Mighels[6] Piper married Gideon Leavitt.

THEIR CHILDREN :

**213.** i. ELIZABETH PIPER[7] LEAVITT (*Betsey Mighels[5] Piper, Elisha[5], Elisha[4], Samuel[3], Samuel[2], Nathaniel[1]*), born March 28, 1822, in Newburgh, Me.; married George Eli Sewell, Nov. 23, 1845, born Nov. 16, 1820, in Frederickton, New Brunswick; a farmer. He died May 1, 1865, in Dixmont, Me., where he resided.

**214.** ii. GIDEON PIPER[7] LEAVITT (*Betsey Mighels[5] Piper, Elisha[5], Elisha[4], Samuel[3], Samuel[2], Nathaniel[1]*), born Dec. 30, 1823, in Newport, Me.; a farmer; married. 1st, Sally Bussy Thomas, Dec., 1850; born in 1830, in Newburgh, Me.; died April 20, 1870, in Newburgh; 2d, Martha Ann Mudgett, Nov. 24, 1870, born Nov. 25, 1832, in Newburgh. He resides in Newburgh.

(**104.**) Ann[6] Piper married George Bickford.

THEIR CHILDREN :

**215.** i. HARRIET LEAVITT[7] BICKFORD (*Ann[6] Piper, Elisha[5], Elisha[4], Samuel[3], Samuel[2], Nathaniel[1]*), born July 19, 1833, in New-

* Although he was born a few weeks before his brother Elisha Franklin[7] Leavitt died, he was not named till after his brother's death.

burgh, Me.; married Enoch Lincoln Bartlett, Oct., 1852, born Oct. 24, 1831, in Newburgh; a farmer. She died May 5, 1860, in Newburgh. He resides in Newburgh.

**216.** ii. GEORGE WASHINGTON⁷ BICKFORD (*Ann⁶ Piper, Elisha⁵, Elisha⁴, Samuel³, Samuel², Nathaniel¹*), born Feb. 15, 1835, in Newburgh, Me.; died Feb., 1842, in Newburgh.

**217.** iii. LENORA MATILLA⁷ BICKFORD (*Ann⁶ Piper, Elisha⁵, Elisha⁴, Samuel³, Samuel², Nathaniel¹*), born Oct. 22, 1836, in Newburgh, Me.; a teacher before marriage; married, as his second wife, Enoch Lincoln Bartlett, May, 1862, born Oct. 24, 1831, in Newburgh; a farmer. He resides in Newburgh.

**218.** iv. HORACE PIPER⁷ BICKFORD (*Ann⁶ Piper, Elisha⁵, Elisha⁴, Samuel³, Samuel², Nathaniel¹*), born March 23, 1839, in Newburgh, Me.; died in 1840, in Newburgh.

**219.** v. WARREN FRANKLIN⁷ BICKFORD (*Ann⁶ Piper, Elisha⁵, Elisha⁴, Samuel³, Samuel², Nathaniel¹*), born Jan. 31, 1842, in Newburgh, Me.; graduated from Bowdoin College in 1872; taught school six months, and then commenced preaching in Feb., 1873. In Sept., 1874, he entered the Theological Seminary at Bangor, Me., and graduated in June, 1876; was installed pastor of the Congregational Church at Winthrop, Me., June 20, 1876, and remained there four years. He resigned in August, 1880, to accept a position in Colorado, under the American Home Missionary Society, where he labored successfully at Breckenridge and Manitou Springs five years. In Sept., 1885, he went to California, and became pastor of Park Church, at Berkeley, where he is now preaching. He married Sarah Wilder, Aug. 15, 1872, daughter of Deacon Horace and Caroline (Jennison) Wilder, of Dixmont, Me. She was born Nov. 8, 1844, in Dixmont, and a teacher before marriage.*

**220.** vi. JESSE PIPER⁷ BICKFORD (*Ann⁶ Piper, Elisha⁵, Elisha⁴, Samuel³, Samuel², Nathaniel¹*), born March 3, 1844, in Newburgh, Me. After his graduation at Bowdoin College, in 1874, he immediately entered upon the business of teaching as a profession. Besides several district schools, he has taught the High School at Monroe, Me.; the Classical Institute at Milton, N. H.; the Lindsey High School at Shapleigh, Me.; and West Lebanon Academy at West Lebanon, Me. He has also taught at La Moure,

---

* Their children are as follows: 1. Mary Perkins, born Feb. 21, 1879, in Winthrop, Me. 2. Warren Franklin, Jr., born Jan. 28, 1887, in Berkeley, Cal.

North Dakota, and is now teaching at Carmel, Me. He has been engaged in teaching almost constantly since he left college. He married Lizzie Horne, July 30, 1876, adopted daughter of James R. Horne, of Milton, N. H. She was born in 1860, in Mass. He resides in Carmel.

**221.** vii. OLDER MICHELS⁷ BICKFORD (*Ann⁶ Piper, Elisha⁵, Elisha⁴, Samuel³, Samuel², Nathaniel¹*), born Oct. 30, 1845, in Newburgh, Me.; a farmer; married Emma Annette Brown, April 12, 1867, born July 18, 1851, in Newburgh, Me. He resides in Newburgh.

**222.** viii. ANNIE ELIZABETH⁷ BICKFORD (*Ann⁶ Piper, Elisha⁵, Elisha⁴, Samuel³, Samuel², Nathaniel¹*), born Oct. 22, 1847, in Newburgh, Me.; a teacher. She resides in Newburgh. I am much indebted to her for furnishing me the genealogies of several of the Piper families in Newburgh.

　(**107.**) Elisha⁶ Piper married Harriet Eurbank.

THEIR CHILDREN :

**223.** i. SAMUEL BURBANK⁷ PIPER (*Elisha⁶, Elisha⁵, Elisha⁴, Samuel³, Samuel². Nathaniel¹*), born May 19, 1835, in Parsonsfield, Me.; died April 23, 1837, in Parsonsfield.

**224.** ii. SAMUEL FULLERTON⁷ PIPER (*Elisha⁶, Elisha⁵, Elisha⁴, Samuel³, Samuel², Nathaniel¹*), born March 11, 1838, in Parsonsfield, Me.; a farmer; married Mary Jane Brigdon, usually called Jennie, daughter of Edmund and Abigail (Nason) Bragdon, Nov. 6, 1865. She was born Oct. 31, 1836, in Limington, Me.; a teacher before marriage. He resides in Parsonsfield on the old homestead of his father and great-grandfather, where he carries on the business of farming successfully, as did his predecessors.—SEE THEIR CHILDREN : Nos. **323, 324.**

**225.** iii. JOHN WESLEY⁷ PIPER (*Elisha⁶, Elisha⁵, Elisha⁴, Samuel³, Samuel², Nathaniel¹*), born Oct. 4, 1839, in Parsonsfield, Me.; a farmer and teacher. He has taught successfully in his own State, Illinois, and Virginia, making in all about eight full school years. He was sent to Virginia as missionary teacher of the freedmen, by the Freewill Baptist Home Missionary Society, in connection with the American Missionary Board, receiving his commission from both societies. He began his work at Staunton, and had charge of over four hundred scholars, being assisted by several female teachers. The people were bitterly opposed to the teachers, but by his judicious management he gained the confidence of some of them,

and was invited to dine with one; and another, a very wealthy
man, desired him to give instruction to his son, which he did, giving him two private lessons each week. He has given considerable attention to music, and been organist for the Freewill Baptist Church, on the South Road in Parsonsfield, twenty-eight years,
and chorister nine. He married Ellen Adelaide Manson, daughter
of George and Emeline (Meads) Manson, Jan. 1, 1867. She was
born April 7, 1845, in Limington, Me.; a teacher before marriage.
He resides in Parsonsfield, on the South Road, on the farm formerly
owned by Jonathan[5] Piper.—SEE HIS CHILD: No. 325.

(127.) Horace[6] Piper married Josephine Fennett Lord.

### THEIR CHILDREN :

228. i. WILLIAM WIRT[7] PIPER (*Horace[6]*, *Jonathan[5]*, *Elisha[4]*,
*Samuel[3]*, *Samuel[2]*, *Nathaniel[1]*), born July 15, 1839, in Limerick,
Me. He completed the English and classical course of study in
Biddeford High School ; studied medicine, and graduated at the
Medical School of Dartmouth College in 1867, receiving the degree
of M. D.; was Assistant Surgeon in the 13th Regt. U. S. Colored
Heavy Artillery, in the Union Army, in the War of the Rebellion.
He was examined and received his appointment before he had fully
completed his medical course ; married Lucinda Cook, Aug. 28,
1875, born July 9, 1845, in Oshtemo, Mich    He resides and prac-
tices medicine in Cleveland, Ohio.  They have no children.

227. ii. HORACE LORD[7] PIPER (*Horace[6]*, *Jonathan[5]*, *Elisha[4]*,
*Samuel[3]*, *Samuel[2]*, *Nathaniel[1]*), born July 14, 1841, in Limerick,
Me. He was one year in Bowdoin College ; Lieutenant in the Union
Army in the War of the Rebellion ; was in the battle of Baylor's
Farm, Va.; of Petersburg, June 15 and 16 and July 18, 1864, and
of the Explosion of the Mine, besides several minor engagements.
He received a medal from Congress for meritorious services in the
war, and was brevetted Major ; graduated at the Law School of
Columbian University, receiving the degree of LL. B.; and was
admitted to the bar in Washington, D. C.   He was also one of the
Commissioners appointed by the United States Government to visit
European ports in order to ascertain the treatment of emigrants to
this country on board of steamboats, with the view of modifying
the laws of emigration, if necessary.   He married Tryphena Stuart
Gove, daughter of Alvan Chadbourne and Mary Susan (Edgerly)

Gove, Oct. 18, 1862, born June 11, 1843, in Limington, Me. He resides in Washington, D. C.—SEE THEIR CHILD : No. **326**.

**228**. iii. MARY JOSEPHINE⁷ PIPER (*Horace⁶, Jonathan⁵, Elisha⁴, Samuel³, Samuel², Nathaniel¹*), born Jan. 25, 1843. in Limerick, Me.; married Oren Hooper, Dec. 7, 1864, son of Noah and Mary (Foss) Hooper, born Dec. 10, 1840, in Biddeford, Me.; a merchant. He commenced business in Limerick, and subsequently removed to Portland, Me., where he now resides, and is carrying on an extensive business in trade. She was a kind daughter and an affectionate wife. Although surrounded with everything to make her happy, she was not permitted to enjoy it long. She died Oct. 5, 1869, in Portland, at the early age of twenty-six years. Of pleasing manners and a gentle spirit, she endeared herself to all, and left precious memories to her surviving friends. She united with the Second Congregational Church of Biddeford several years before her death.--SEE THEIR CHILDREN : Nos. **327, 328, 329**.

(**122**.) Irving⁶ Piper married, 1st, Mary Emery ; 2d, Elizabeth Chase.

THEIR CHILD :

**229**. i. SHERMAN EMERY⁷ PIPER (*Irving⁶, Jonathan⁵, Elisha⁴, Samuel³, Samuel², Nathaniel¹*), born Jan. 28, 1847, in Parsonsfield, Me.; a farmer, teacher, land-surveyor, and trustee of Parsonsfield Seminary. He has taught school several years in different places with good success ; married Minnie Charlotte Black, daughter of Jacob and Charlotte (Swett) Black, May 1, 1878. She was born Jan. 28, 1849, in Limington, Me.; taught school for a long time before marriage, and was assistant teacher in Parsonsfield Seminary. She excelled as a reader, and gave lessons in elocution. He resides in Parsonsfield near Parsonsfield Seminary, on the homestead of his father and grandfather.--SEE THEIR CHILDREN : Nos. **330, 331**.

(**123**.) Catharine Redman⁶ Piper married Abram Fogg Marston.

THEIR CHILDREN :

**230**. i. MARY LUCRETIA⁷ MARSTON (*Catharine Redman⁶ Piper, Jonathan⁵, Elisha⁴, Samuel³, Samuel², Nathaniel¹*), born July 6, 1848, in Effingham, N. H.; married Francis Weston Barker, Nov. 17, 1872, born April 17, 1846, in Lovell, Me.; a farmer, teacher, superintending school committee, selectman, and soldier in the

Union Army in the War of the Rebellion. He was in the battles of North Anna River, Cold Harbor, Petersburg, June 15, 1864; the Explosion of the Mine at Petersburg, July 30, 1864; Poplar Grove Church, Sept. 30, 1864, and the Capture of Petersburg, April 2, 1865. He resides in Effingham, N. H.*

**231.** ii. JOHN PIPER⁷ MARSTON (*Catharine Redman⁶ Piper, Jonathan⁵, Elisha⁴, Samuel³, Samuel², Nathaniel¹*), born July 19, 1850, in Effingham, N. H. He graduated at Bates College in 1873, and immediately engaged in the business of teaching, which he has pursued thirteen years, with marked success. Besides other schools he taught Wiscasset High School three years; Bath High School four years, Rockland High School five, and is now (1889) Principal of Biddeford High School. He married Alice Guyletta Swett, Aug. 4, 1880, born May 31, 1859, in Bucksport, Me. He resides in Biddeford, Me..

### EIGHTH GENERATION.

(**144.**) Lorenzo Dow⁷ Piper married Mary Jane Nason.

THEIR CHILDREN:

**232.** i. IDA WALLINGFORD⁸ PIPER (*Lorenzo Dow⁷, Benjamin⁶, Benjamin⁵, Elisha⁴, Samuel³, Samuel², Nathaniel¹*), born May 27, 1851, in Berwick, Me.; married John Torsleff, Dec. 18, 1872, born Oct. 12, 1844, in Boston, Mass.; a farmer. He resides in West Mitchell, Iowa.—SEE THEIR CHILD: No. **332.**

**233.** ii. MARY WALLINGFORD⁸ PIPER (*Lorenzo Dow⁷, Benjamin⁶, Benjamin⁵, Elisha⁴, Samuel³, Samuel², Nathaniel¹*), born Jan. 18, 1857, in Berwick, Me.; married Robert Waddell, Sept. 17, 1879, born June 23, 1847, in Scotland; a farmer. He resides in West Mitchell, Iowa.—SEE THEIR CHILD: No. **333.**

(**145.**) Joseph Perkins⁷ Piper married Ann Maria Frost.

THEIR CHILDREN:

**234.** i. FREDDY WILDER⁸ PIPER (*Joseph Perkins⁷, Benjamin⁶, Benjamin⁵, Elisha⁴, Samuel³, Samuel², Nathaniel¹*), born July 16, 1853, in Parsonsfield, Me.; died Nov. 16, 1859, in Parsonsfield.

**235.** ii. SARAH JANE⁸ PIPER (*Joseph Perkins⁷, Benjamin⁶, Benjamin⁵, Elisha⁴, Samuel³, Samuel², Nathaniel¹*), born July 10, 1855, in Parsonsfield, Me.

---

* They have one child, Kate Eugenie, born Nov. 6, 1873, in Effingham, N. H.

(**146.**) Charles Abbott⁷ Piper married Mary Emeline Hall.

THEIR CHILDREN :

**236.** i. PERLEY WESLEY⁸ PIPER (*Charles Abbott⁷*, *Benjamin⁶*, *Benjamin⁵*, *Elisha⁴*, *Samuel³*, *Samuel²*, *Nathaniel¹*), born Jan. 29, 1856, in Parsonsfield, Me.; died Feb. 26, 1857, in Parsonsfield.

**237.** ii. PERLEY WESLEY⁸ PIPER (*Charles Abbott⁷*, *Benjamin⁶*, *Benjamin⁵*, *Elisha⁴*, *Samuel³*, *Samuel²*, *Nathaniel¹*), born Feb. 21, 1857, in Parsonsfield, Me.; died Dec. 22, 1858, in Parsonsfield.

**238.** iii. MARSIS⁸ PIPER (*Charles Abbott⁷*, *Benjamin⁶*, *Benjamin⁵*, *Elisha⁴*, *Samuel³*, *Samuel²*, *Nathaniel¹*), born May 27, 1861, in Parsonsfield, Me.; died July 28, 1861, in Parsonsfield.

**239.** iv. GEORGE HENRY⁸ PIPER (*Charles Abbott⁷*, *Benjamin⁶*, *Benjamin⁵*, *Elisha⁴*, *Samuel³*, *Samuel²*, *Nathaniel¹*), born March 9, 1864, in Parsonsfield, Me.; a clerk. He resides in Biddeford.

**240.** v. EDWARD EVERETT⁸ PIPER (*Charles Abbott⁷*, *Benjamin⁶*, *Benjamin⁵*, *Elisha⁴*, *Samuel³*, *Samuel²*, *Nathaniel¹*), born Sept. 29, 1866, in Parsonsfield, Me.; a book-keeper. He excels in penmanship. His residence is in Portland, Me.

**241.** vi. ALVAH CHESSMAN⁸ PIPER (*Charles Abbott⁷*, *Benjamin⁶*, *Benjamin⁵*, *Elisha⁴*, *Samuel³*, *Samuel²*, *Nathaniel¹*), born Dec. 11, 1869, in Parsonsfield, Me. He resides in North Berwick, Me.

(**154.**) Perry H.⁷ Piper married Harriet Hart Savage.

THEIR CHILDREN :

**242.** i. DOROTHY⁸ PIPER (*Perry H.⁷*, *Ezekiel⁶*, *David⁵*, *Elisha⁴*, *Samuel³*, *Samuel²*, *Nathaniel¹*), born Jan. 16, 1844, in Hollowayville, Ill.; died March 10, 1846, in Hollowayville.

**243.** ii. WARREN TAYLOR⁸ PIPER (*Perry H.⁷*, *Ezekiel⁶*, *David⁵*, *Elisha⁴*, *Samuel³*, *Samuel²*, *Nathaniel¹*), born Jan. 13, 1846, in Hollowayville, Ill.; a farmer ; married Elizabeth Marlatt, Aug. 31, 1866, born June 17, 1848, in Warren, New Jersey. He resides in Malden, Ill.—SEE THEIR CHILD : No. **334.**

**244.** iii. CHARLOTTE⁸ PIPER (*Perry H.⁷*, *Ezekiel⁶*, *David⁵*, *Elisha⁴*, *Samuel³*, *Samuel²*, *Nathaniel¹*), born Oct. 16, 1854, in Hollowayville, Ill.; married Joseph Johnston, March, 1872, born Dec. 19, 1847, in Malden, Ill.; a farmer. He resides in Princeton, Ill. —SEE THEIR CHILDREN : Nos. **335, 336.**

**245.** iv. MORGAN HIRAM⁸ PIPER (*Perry H.⁷*, *Ezekiel⁶*, *David⁵*, *Elisha⁴*, *Samuel³*, *Samuel²*, *Nathaniel¹*), born Feb. 19, 1856, in Hollowayville, Ill.; a farmer ; married Honora Litchfield, Nov. 1,

1877, born Sept. 5, 1858, in De Pue, Ill. He resides in Vinton, Iowa.—SEE THEIR CHILDREN : Nos. **337, 338, 339, 340.**

(**155.**) David⁷ Piper married Philipina Heintz.

THEIR CHILDREN :

**246.** i. LAWRENCE⁸ PIPER (*David⁷, Ezekiel⁶, David⁵, Elisha⁴, Samuel³, Samuel², Nathaniel¹*), born Oct. 31, 1849, in Hollowayville, Ill.; died Mar. 28, 1851, in Hollowayville.

**247.** ii. MARY LAVINIA⁸ PIPER (*David⁷, Ezekiel⁶, David⁵, Elisha⁴, Samuel³, Samuel², Nathaniel¹*), born Aug. 28, 1851, in Hollowayville, Ill.; married George Monroe Minier, Feb. 18, 1877, born Dec. 26, 1848, in Leepertown, Ill.; a farmer. He resides in Tiskilwa, Ill.—SEE THEIR CHILDREN : Nos. **341, 342, 343, 344.**

**248.** iii. EZEKIEL⁸ PIPER (*David⁷, Ezekiel⁶, David⁵, Elisha⁴, Samuel³, Samuel², Nathaniel¹*), born Jan. 9, 1854, in Hollowayville, Ill.; a farmer; married Mary Elizabeth Harris, March 14, 1878, born Sept. 23, 1859. in Dimmock, Ill. He resides in Tiskilwa, Ill.—SEE THEIR CHILDREN : Nos. **345, 346, 347.**

**249.** iv. EDWARD⁸ PIPER (*David⁷, Ezekiel⁶, David⁵, Elisha⁴, Samuel³, Samuel², Nathaniel¹*), born Aug. 28, 1856, in Hollowayville, Ill.; a farmer ; married Jennie Warson, March 13, 1883. born Nov. 23, 1860, in Branchton, Canada. He died March 24, 1888, in Tiskilwa, Ill., where he resided. They had no children.

**250.** v. KATE⁸ PIPER (*David⁷, Ezekiel⁶, David⁵, Elisha⁴, Samuel³, Samuel², Nathaniel¹*), born Dec. 6, 1860, in Hollowayville, Ill.; married John Marlatt, Feb. 11, 1887, born July 24, 1852, in Warren, New Jersey ; a farmer. He resides in Nortonville, Kans. They have no children.

(**156.**) Marinda⁷ Piper married Frederick Heintz.

THEIR CHILDREN :

**251.** i. KATE⁸ HEINTZ (*Marinda⁷ Piper, Ezekiel⁶, David⁵, Elisha⁴, Samuel³, Samuel², Nathaniel¹*), born Dec. 1, 1844, in Selby, Ill ; married Isaac Adolphus Watson, Nov. 25. 1879, born May, 1844, in Chicago, Ill.; express messenger on railroad. He resides in Chicago.*

**252.** ii. FETNAH⁸ HEINTZ (*Marinda⁷ Piper. Ezekiel⁶. David⁵, Elisha⁴, Samuel³, Samuel², Nathaniel¹*), born March 5, 1846, in Selby, Ill.; married Leander White, Aug. 21, 1862, born March

*They have one child, Frederick, born Sept. 14, 1882, in Chicago, Ill.

29, 1838, in Batavia, Ohio; a farmer. He resides in Selby, Ill.*

**253.** iii. HENRY HEINTZ⁸ (*Marinda⁷ Piper, Ezekiel², David⁵, Elisha⁴, Samuel³, Samuel², Nathaniel¹*), born June 1, 1849, in Selby, Ill.; married Martha Snyder, Aug. 17, 1869, born Aug. 17, 1851, in Hall, Ill. He resides in Princeton, Ill.†

**254.** iv. ANNA TRUMP⁸ HEINTZ (*Marinda⁷ Piper, Ezekiel⁶, David⁵, Elisha⁴, Samuel³, Samuel², Nathaniel¹*), born Sept. 10, 1858, in Selby, Ill.; a stenographic reporter. She resides in Boston, Mass.

(**157.**) Hiram Harding⁷ Piper married Mary Amanda McWilliams.

THEIR CHILDREN :

**255.** i. VIOLA ANN⁸ PIPER (*Hiram Harding⁷, Ezekiel⁶, David⁵, Elisha⁴, Samuel³, Samuel², Nathaniel¹*), born Nov. 23, 1860, in Malden, Ill.; married William Sidwell Mercer, Feb. 5, 1880, born July 10, 1857, in Malden, Ill.; a farmer. He resides in Malden. —SEE THEIR CHILDREN : Nos. **348, 349.**

**256.** ii. MARY LAVINIA⁸ PIPER (*Hiram Harding⁷, Ezekiel⁶, David⁵, Elisha⁴, Samuel³, Samuel², Nathaniel¹*), born Oct. 14, 1862, in Malden, Ill., where she resides.

**257.** iii. MARGARET⁸ PIPER (*Hiram Harding⁷, Ezekiel⁶, David⁵, Elisha⁴, Samuel³, Samuel², Nathaniel¹*), born Jan. 13, 1864, in Malden, Ill., where she resides.

**258.** iv. ABRAHAM LINCOLN⁸ PIPER (*Hiram Harding⁷, Ezekiel⁶, David⁵, Elisha⁴, Samuel³, Samuel², Nathaniel¹*), born Jan. 6, 1866, in Malden, Ill.; a farmer; married Iona Belle Mercer, July 3, 1884,

---

* Their children are as follows : 1. Frank, born June 28, 1866, in Hall, Ill. 2. Frederick, born April 20, 1868, in Hall. 3. David, born March 14, 1870, in Hall. 4. Mary, born June 6, 1873, in Hall. 5. Henry, born April 23, 1876, in Los Nietos, Cal. 6. Jessie, born Jan. 11, 1879, in Los Nietos. 7. Winfield, born Dec. 3, 1882, in Selby, Ill. 8. Edward C., born Oct. 19, 1884, in Selby. 9. Annie, born Sept. 19, 1886, in Selby ; died Feb. 22, 1887. 10. Abbie, born Sept. 19, 1886, in Selby ; died March 7, 1887. She and her sister Annie were twins.

† Their children : 1. Cora, born April 12, 1871, in Nemaha County, Neb. 2. Frederick, born Sept. 25, 1872, in Selby, Ill. 3. Alma Nancy, born March 20, 1874, in Hall, Ill. 4. Annie Marinda, born July 17, 1875, in Hall. 5. Flora, born June 16, 1877, in Selby. 6. Blanche, born Oct. 30, 1879, in Dover, Ill.; died in August, 1881, in Dover.

born June 26, 1864. in Malden, Ill. She died April 27, 1888, in Malden. He resides in Malden. They had no children.

**259.** v. June Hiram⁸ Piper (*Hiram Harding⁷*, *Ezekiel⁶*, *David⁵ Elisha⁴*, *Samuel³*, *Samuel²*, *Nathaniel¹*), born Dec. 27, 1868, in Malden, Ill. He resides in Malden.

**260.** vi. William Ezekiel⁸ Piper (*Hiram Harding⁷*, *Ezekiel⁶*, *David⁵*, *Elisha⁴*, *Samuel³*, *Samuel²*, *Nathaniel¹*), born Feb. 28, 1870, in Malden, Ill., where he resides.

**261.** vii. David Ansel⁸ Piper (*Hiram Harding⁷*, *Ezekiel⁶*, *David⁵*, *Elisha⁴*, *Samuel³*, *Samuel²*, *Nathaniel¹*), born Dec. 23, 1871, in Malden, Ill., where he resides.

**262.** viii. John⁸ Piper (*Hiram Harding⁷*, *Ezekiel⁶*, *David⁵*, *Elisha⁴*, *Samuel³*, *Samuel²*, *Nathaniel¹*). born July 15, 1873. in Malden, Ill. He died Oct. 14, 1874, in Malden.

**263.** ix. Albert⁸ Piper (*Hiram Harding⁷*, *Ezekiel⁶*, *David⁵*, *Elisha⁴*. *Samuel³*, *Samuel²*, *Nathaniel¹*), born April 1, 1875, in Malden, Ill.

**264.** x. Harding⁸ Piper (*Hiram Harding⁷*, *Ezekiel⁶*, *David⁵*, *Elisha⁴*, *Samuel³*, *Samuel²*, *Nathaniel¹*). born Aug. 7, 1876, in Malden. Ill.

(**159.**) Mary Ann⁷ Piper married William Simon Dalton.

THEIR CHILDREN :

**265.** i. Naomi⁸ Dalton (*Mary Ann⁷ Piper*, *Ezekiel⁶*, *David⁵*, *Elisha⁴*, *Samuel³*, *Samuel²*, *Nathaniel¹*), born July 7, 1857, in Malden, Ill.; died July 16, 1863, in Malden.

**266.** ii. Hiram James⁸ Dalton (*Mary Ann⁷ Piper*, *Ezekiel⁶*, *David⁵*, *Elisha⁴*, *Samuel³*, *Samuel²*, *Nathaniel¹*). born Aug. 5, 1860, in Malden, Ill.; a farmer. He resides in Malden.

**267.** iii. Elmer⁸ Dalton (*Mary Ann⁷ Piper*, *Ezekiel⁶*, *David⁵*. *Elisha⁴*, *Samuel³*, *Samuel²*, *Nathaniel¹*). born Nov. 25, 1862, in Malden, Ill.; died March 11, 1877, in Malden.

**268.** iv. William⁸ Dalton (*Mary Ann⁷ Piper*, *Ezekiel⁶*, *David⁵*, *Elisha⁴*, *Samuel³*, *Samuel²*, *Nathaniel¹*). born Nov. 28, 1864, in Malden, Ill ; a farmer ; married Mary Ann Charles, Aug. 28, 1883, born Nov. 12, 1862, at Bureau Junction, Ill. He resides in Princeton, Ill.

**269.** v. Lillie May⁸ Dalton (*Mary Ann⁷ Piper*, *Ezekiel⁶*, *David⁵*, *Elisha⁴*, *Samuel³*. *Samuel²*, *Nathaniel¹*), born Sept. 23, 1866, in Malden, Ill.; married Lesliner Pierce, Feb. 4. 1886, born Nov. 16, 1867, in Dover, Ill.; a farmer. He resides in Wheeler, Iowa.

**270.** vi. ELENDER[8] DALTON (*Mary Ann[7] Piper, Ezekiel[6], David[5], Elisha[4], Samuel[3], Samuel[2], Nathaniel[1]*), born Oct. 26, 1869, in Malden, Ill.; died Jan. 28, 1870, in Malden.

**271.** vii. ANNIE ELENDER[8] DALTON (*Mary Ann[7] Piper, Ezekiel[6], David[5], Elisha[4], Samuel[3], Samuel[2], Nathaniel[1]*), born Oct. 26, 1869, in Malden, Ill., where she resides. She and her sister Elender Dalton were twins.

(**159.**) Lavinia Harding[7] Piper married Jonathan Oglesbee.

THEIR CHILDREN :

**272.** i. RUTH[8] OGLESBEE (*Lavinia Harding[7] Piper, Ezekiel[6], David[5], Elisha[4], Samuel[3], Samuel[2], Nathaniel[1]*), born Jan. 25, 1860, in Princeton, Ill.; died Dec. 15, 1877, in Memphis, Tenn. She resided in Harveysburg, Ohio.

**273.** ii. ELIAS[8] OGLESBEE (*Lavinia Harding[7] Piper, Ezekiel[6], David[5], Elisha[4], Samuel[3], Samuel[2], Nathaniel[1]*), born May 10, 1862, in Harveysburg, Ohio , a farmer ; married Lida Sabilla Sears, Sept. 24, 1887, born Aug. 1, 1863, in Harveysburg. He resides in Harveysburg.

**274.** iii. MARY LAVINIA[8] OGLESBEE (*Lavinia Harding[7] Piper, Ezekiel[6], David[5], Elisha[4], Samuel[3], Samuel[2], Nathaniel[1]*), born Sept. 28, 1863, in Harveysburg, Ohio ; married George Evans Watson, Nov. 21, 1883, born Jan. 22, 1862, in Malden, Ill.; a farmer. He resides in Malden.

(**163.**) William Wilkinson[7] Piper married, 1st, Lydia Ann Savage ; 2d, Cordelia Barrett.

THEIR CHILDREN :

**275.** i. FLORENCE AMANDA[8] PIPER (*William Wilkinson[7], Ezekiel[6], David[5], Elisha[4], Samuel[3], Samuel[2], Nathaniel[1]*), born April 9, 1858, in Selby, Ill.; married Thomas William Griffin, Dec. 12, 1876, born Aug. 21, 1843, in Princeton, Ill.; a farmer. He resides in Princeton.—SEE THEIR CHILD : No. **350.**

**276.** ii. VICTOR WILLIAM[8] PIPER (*William Wilkinson[7], Ezekiel[6], David[5], Elisha[4], Samuel[3], Samuel[2], Nathaniel[1]*), born Sept. 7, 1860, in Selby, Ill.; died July 22, 1863, in Selby.

**277.** iii. OWEN JERSEY[8] PIPER (*William Wilkinson[7], Ezekiel[6], David[5], Elisha[4], Samuel[3], Samuel[2], Nathaniel[1]*), born Feb. 8, 1866, in Selby, Ill.; a farmer ; married Nancy Self, Feb. 10, 1886, born Dec. 2, 1867, in Berlin, Ill. He resides in Princeton, Ill. They have no children.

(163.) Mary Ann⁷ Piper married John Guilford Combs.

**278.** i. GEORGE WEEKS⁸ COMBS (*Mary Ann⁷ Piper, Elisha⁶, David⁵, Elisha⁴, Samuel³, Samuel², Nathaniel¹*), born Jan. 28, 1850, in Hall, Ill.; a farmer.  He resides in Buda, Ill.

**279.** ii. HOWARD MILTON⁸ COMBS (*Mary Ann⁷ Piper, Elisha⁶, David⁵, Elisha⁴, Samuel³, Samuel², Nathaniel¹*), born Dec. 3, 1852, in Hall, Ill.; a farmer.  He resides in Adams County, Ill.

**280.** iii. AMELIA JANE⁸ COMBS (*Mary Ann⁷ Piper, Elisha⁶, David⁵, Elisha⁴, Samuel³, Samuel², Nathaniel¹*), born May 22, 1855, in Hall, Ill.; married J. E. Ross, Feb. 17, 1885.  He resides in Bedford, Iowa.

**281.** iv. OSCAR LEMON⁸ COMBS (*Mary Ann⁷ Piper, Elisha⁶, David⁵, Elisha⁴, Samuel³, Samuel², Nathaniel¹*), born Sept. 27, 1857, in Hall, Ill.; a farmer ; died Oct. 28, 1882, in Hall, where he resided.

**282.** v. WILLIAM ELLERY⁸ COMBS (*Mary Ann⁷ Piper, Elisha⁶, David⁵, Elisha⁴, Samuel³, Samuel², Nathaniel¹*), born June 29, 1864, in Hall, Ill.; a farmer. . He resides in Auburn, Neb.

(166.) Caroline⁷ Piper married Francis Marion Long.

**283.** i. HENRY CLINTON⁸ LONG (*Caroline⁷ Piper, Elisha⁶, David⁵, Elisha⁴, Samuel³, Samuel², Nathaniel¹*), born May 16, 1854, in Selby, Ill.; a farmer.  He resides at Fort Yates, North Dakota.

**284.** ii. MARY ANN⁸ LONG (*Caroline⁷ Piper, Elisha⁶, David⁵, Elisha⁴, Samuel³, Samuel², Nathaniel¹*), born July 5, 1856, in Selby, Ill.; married Benjamin Franklin Searl, Oct. 7, 1875, born Sept. 7, 1853, in Selby, Ill.; a farmer.  He resides in Selby.

**285.** iii. ALBERT CHARLES⁸ LONG (*Caroline⁷ Piper, Elisha⁶, David⁵, Elisha⁴, Samuel³, Samuel², Nathaniel¹*), born Jan. 8, 1859, in Selby, Ill.; a farmer ; married Margaret Welsh, Nov. 22, 1884, born Nov. 13, 1864, in Lawrence County, N. Y.  He resides in Hastings, Neb.

**286.** iv. ALMA CONNOR⁸ LONG (*Caroline⁷ Piper, Elisha⁶, David⁵, Elisha⁴, Samuel³, Samuel², Nathaniel¹*), born Jan. 8, 1859, in Selby, Ill.  She and her brother Albert are twins.  She married Joseph Frederick Grissible, Oct. 7, 1875, born Oct. 7 1853, in Selby, Ill.; a farmer.  He resides in Anita, Iowa.

(**170.**) Albert Parsons⁷ Piper married, 1st, Abby Richards Towle ; 2d, Maria Arnold Vose.

THEIR CHILDREN :

**287.** i. Charles Albert⁸ Piper (*Albert Parsons⁷, Thomas Parsons⁶, Daniel⁵, Elisha⁴, Samuel³, Samuel², Nathaniel¹*), born March 9, 1854, in Monroe, Me.; a box-maker. He resides in Lowell, Mass.

**288.** ii. Marilla Mason⁸ Piper (*Albert Parsons⁷, Thomas Parsons⁶, Daniel⁵. Elisha⁴, Samuel³, Samuel², Nathaniel¹*), born June 12, 1875, in Thomaston, Me. This child was by his second wife, whom he married in 1872.

(**174.**) Susan Bickford⁷ Piper married Byron Porter.

THEIR CHILD :

**289.** i. Martin Luther⁸ Porter (*Susan Bickford⁷ Piper, Benjamin⁶. Daniel⁵. Elisha⁴, Samuel³, Samuel², Nathaniel¹*), born Sept. 19, 1859, in Dixmont, Me.; a physician ; married Clara Annie Quimby, April 29, 1882. born in Topsfield, Me., Dec. 31, 1855 ; a teacher before marriage. He graduated at the Medical Department of the University of Vermont in July, 1880, receiving the degree of M. D., and immediately entered upon the practice of his profession in Danforth, Me., where he has an extensive business as a physician and surgeon. Since 1882 he has been United States Examining Surgeon for pensions. He is also a member of the Penobscot County Medical Society, and of the New Brunswick Council of Physicians and Surgeons.

(**175.**) Daniel⁷ Piper married Helen Wildes.

THEIR CHILDREN :

**290.** i. Arthur Benson⁸ Piper (*Daniel⁷, Benjamin⁶, Daniel⁵, Elisha⁴, Samuel³, Samuel², Nathaniel¹*), born Oct. 8, 1859, in Monroe, Me.; a mariner, being first mate of a large merchant-ship. His residence is in Dixmont, Me.

**291.** ii. Allen Hamlin⁸ Piper (*Daniel⁷, Benjamin⁶, Daniel⁵, Elisha⁴, Samuel³, Samuel², Nathaniel¹*), born June 20, 1861, in Monroe, Me.; a farmer. He resides in Dixmont, Me.

**292.** iii. Grace Marie⁸ Piper (*Daniel⁷, Benjamin⁶, Daniel⁵, Elisha⁴, Samuel³, Samuel², Nathaniel¹*), born Jan. 29, 1864, in Monroe, Me.; married Willis Fletcher, Oct. 5, 1884, born Aug. 9, 1862, in Dixmont, Me.; a machinist. She died March 20, 1888, in Dixmont. He resides in Lowell, Mass.

**293.** iv. MABEL GERTRUDE[5] PIPER (*Daniel[7]*, *Benjamin[6]*, *Daniel[5]*, *Elisha[4]*, *Samuel[3]*, *Samuel[2]*, *Nathaniel[1]*), born Oct. 20, 1868, in Dixmont, Me.; died March 3, 1870, in Dixmont.

(**180.**) Elisha Sanborn[7] Piper married Eliza Jane Smith.

THEIR CHILDREN:

**294.** i. SARAH FRANCES[8] PIPER (*Elisha Sanborn[7]*, *Elisha[6]*, *Daniel[5]*, *Elisha[4]*, *Samuel[3]*, *Samuel[2]*, *Nathaniel[1]*), born Aug. 11, 1857, in Newburgh, Me.; died May 16, 1866, in Bradley, Me.

**295.** ii. GEORGE ERNEST[8] PIPER (*Elisha Sanborn[7]*, *Elisha[6]*, *Daniel[5]*, *Elisha[4]*, *Samuel[3]*, *Samuel[2]*, *Nathaniel[1]*), born June 22, 1859, in Newburgh, Me.; died May 16, 1866, in Bradley, Me. He and his sister, Sarah Frances, both died the same day. The little innocents wandered from their home unnoticed, their mother being sick abed that day, to the bank of the Penobscot river, which was near by—perhaps to gather flowers at the water's edge, or to dabble in the stream—and both fell in and were drowned. Whether the younger fell in first, and the other attempted to rescue him, or both fell in together, is unknown, for no one saw them when they went to the river, nor when they were drowned.

**296.** iii. FREDERICK WARNER[8] PIPER (*Elisha Sanborn[7]*, *Elisha[6]*, *Daniel[5]*, *Elisha[4]*, *Samuel[3]*, *Samuel[2]*, *Nathaniel[1]*), born Sept. 10, 1863, in Newburgh, Me.; a clerk. He resides in Boston, Mass.

**297.** iv. PEARL FRANCES[8] PIPER (*Elisha Sanborn[7]*, *Elisha[6]*, *Daniel[5]*, *Elisha[4]*, *Samuel[3]*, *Samuel[2]*, *Nathaniel[1]*), born Oct. 10, 1867, in Bradley, Me. She resides in Medford, Mass.

**298.** v. EDITH BELLE[8] PIPER (*Elisha Sanborn[7]*, *Elisha[6]*, *Daniel[5]*, *Elisha[4]*, *Samuel[3]*, *Samuel[2]*, *Nathaniel[1]*), born Feb. 16, 1873, in Medford, Mass.

(**181.**) Enoch Franklin[7] Piper married Adella Whitcomb.

THEIR CHILDREN:

**299.** i. HENRY FRANKLIN[8] PIPER (*Enoch Franklin[7]*, *Elisha[6]*, *Daniel[5]*, *Elisha[4]*, *Samuel[3]*, *Samuel[2]*, *Nathaniel[1]*), born April 1, 1861, in Newburgh, Me. He resides in Lowell, Mass.

**300.** ii. CHARLES SUMNER[8] PIPER (*Enoch Franklin[7]*, *Elisha[6]*, *Daniel[5]*, *Elisha[4]*, *Samuel[3]*, *Samuel[2]*, *Nathaniel[1]*), born Aug. 31, 1872, in Dixmont, Me.

**301.** iii. ADELLA EMMA[8] PIPER (*Enoch Franklin[7]*, *Elisha[6]*, *Daniel[5]*, *Elisha[4]*, *Samuel[3]*, *Samuel[2]*, *Nathaniel[1]*), born Oct. 24, 1881, in Dixmont, Me.

**262.** iv. VIVIAN ANGIE³ PIPER (*Enoch Franklin⁷, Elisha⁶, Daniel⁵, Elisha⁴, Samuel³, Samuel², Nathaniel¹*), born Sept. 13, 1883, in Dixmont, Me.

(**183.**) Rhoda Addie⁷ Piper married William Henry Hollis.

THEIR CHILDREN :

**393.** i. ANGIE⁸ HOLLIS (*Rhoda Addie⁷ Piper, Elisha⁶, Daniel⁵, Elisha⁴, Samuel³, Samuel², Nathaniel¹*), born March 9, 1868, in Newburgh, Me. I am much indebted to her for her assistance in collecting the genealogies of the Piper family. She married Frank Henry McLaughlin, March 22, 1888, born Sept. 26, 1863, in Carmel, Me.; a teacher. He resides in Newburgh.

**394.** ii. CHARLES⁸ HOLLIS (*Rhoda Addie⁷ Piper, Elisha⁶, Daniel⁵, Elisha⁴, Samuel³, Samuel², Nathaniel¹*), born June 24, 1874, in Newburgh, Me.

(**184.**) Susan Emma⁷ Piper married Samuel Woodman Bridgham.

THEIR CHILDREN :

**305.** i. CORA AVIS⁸ BRIDGHAM (*Susan Emma⁷ Piper, Elisha⁶, Daniel⁵, Elisha⁴, Samuel³, Samuel², Nathaniel¹*), born May 18, 1867, in Newburgh, Me.; married Harry Joseph Newhall, Sept. 4, 1888, born May 17, 1862, in Medford, Mass. He is a gold-beater, and resides in Medford.

**306.** ii. MERRITT⁸ BRIDGHAM (*Susan Emma⁷ Piper, Elisha⁶, Daniel⁵, Elisha⁴, Samuel³, Samuel², Nathaniel¹*), born Jan 6, 1869, in Newburgh, Me.; a clerk. He resides in Newburgh.

**307.** iii. EDDIE LUE⁸ BRIDGHAM (*Susan Emma⁷ Piper, Elisha⁶, Daniel⁵, Elisha⁴, Samuel³, Samuel², Nathaniel¹*), born Nov. 22, 1873, in Newburgh, Me.

(**189.**) Eliza Ann⁷ Piper married Brackett Tobias Lord.

THEIR CHILDREN ;

**308.** i. GEORGE⁸ LORD (*Eliza Ann⁷ Piper, Daniel⁶, Daniel⁵, Elisha⁴, Samuel³, Samuel², Nathaniel¹*), born Nov. 8, 1873, in Parsonsfield, Me.

**309.** ii. ELIZA HANNAH⁸ LORD (*Eliza Ann⁷ Piper, Daniel⁶, Daniel⁵, Elisha⁴, Samuel³, Samuel², Nathaniel¹*), born March 7, 1884. in Parsonsfield, Me.

(**190.**) Frederick Augustus[7] Piper married Aurora Low.

THEIR CHILD :

**310.** i. ERNEST LOW[8] PIPER (*Frederick Augustus[7], Simeon Barker[6], Daniel[5], Elisha[4], Samuel[3], Samuel[2], Nathaniel[1]*), born March 21, 1879, in Monroe, Me.

(**192.**) Simeon Barker[7] Piper married Maria Elizabeth Wheeler.

THEIR CHILDREN :

**311.** i. WARREN LLEWELLYN[8] PIPER (*Simeon Barker[7], Simeon Barker[6], Daniel[5], Elisha[4], Samuel[3], Samuel[2], Nathaniel[1]*), born Jan. 18, 1874, in Somerville, N. J.

**312.** ii. WINFRED WILDES[8] PIPER (*Simeon Barker[7], Simeon Barker[6], Daniel[5], Elisha[4], Samuel[3], Samuel[2], Nathaniel[1]*), born Jan. 18, 1878, in Elizabeth, N. J.

**313.** iii. EDWIN FRANCIS[8] PIPER (*Simeon Barker[7], Simeon Barker[6], Daniel[5], Elisha[4], Samuel[3], Samuel[2], Nathaniel[1]*), born Dec. 31, 1882, in Washington, D. C.

(**193.**) Helen Augusta[7] Piper married Peter Cooper.

THEIR CHILDREN :

**314.** i. ELLIS WILDES[8] COOPER (*Helen Augusta[7] Piper, Simeon Barker[6], Daniel[5], Elisha[4], Samuel[3], Samuel[2], Nathaniel[1]*), born Dec. 29, 1878, in Elizabeth, N. J.

**315.** ii. HERBERT ROMEYN[8] COOPER (*Helen Augusta[7] Piper, Simeon Barker[6], Daniel[5], Elisha[4], Samuel[3], Samuel[2], Nathaniel[1]*), born May 29, 1881, in Elizabeth, N. J.

(**195.**) Wyman Brown[7] Piper married Annie Cole Russell.

THEIR CHILDREN :

**316.** i. MAUDE LILLIAN[8] PIPER (*Wyman Brown[7], Alpheus Felch[6], Daniel[5], Elisha[4], Samuel[3], Samuel[2], Nathaniel[1]*), born June 7, 1878, in Corinna, Me.

**317.** ii. PEARL[8] PIPER (*Wyman Brown[7], Alpheus Felch[6], Daniel[5], Elisha[4], Samuel[3], Samuel[2], Nathaniel[1]*), born July 17, 1882, in Corinna, Me.; died Oct. 14, 1882, in Corinna.

(**196.**) Lizzie May[7] Piper married Joseph Granville Patterson.

THEIR CHILD :

**318.** i. JOSIE EVELYN[8] PATTERSON (*Lizzie May[7] Piper, Alpheus Felch[6], Daniel[5], Elisha[4], Samuel[3], Samuel[2], Nathaniel[1]*), born May 28, 1879, in Swanville, Me.

(**200.**) Elisha Franklin[7] Piper married, 1st, Edith Snow ;
2d, Sabra Reed.

THEIR CHILDREN :

**319.** i. MAMIE EMMA[8] PIPER (*Elisha Franklin[7]*, *John Usher
Parsons[6]*, *Daniel[5]*, *Elisha[4]*, *Samuel[3]*, *Samuel[2]*, *Nathaniel[1]*), born
Sept. 18, 1872, in Newburgh, Me.

**320.** ii. WALTER[8] PIPER (*Elisha Franklin[7]*, *John Usher Parsons[6]*, *Daniel[5]*, *Elisha[4]*, *Samuel[3]*, *Samuel[2]*, *Nathaniel[1]*), born Oct.
17, 1874, in Newburgh, Me.

**321.** iii. JOHN HENRY[8] PIPER (*Elisha Franklin[7]*, *John Usher
Parsons[6]*, *Daniel[5]*, *Elisha[4]*, *Samuel[3]*, *Samuel[2]*, *Nathaniel[1]*), born
Oct. 20, 1876, in Dixmont, Me.

**322.** iv. EARL CHESTER[8] PIPER (*Elisha Franklin[7]*, *John Usher
Parsons[6]*, *Daniel[5]*, *Elisha[4]*, *Samuel[3]*, *Samuel[2]*, *Nathaniel[1]*), born
Dec. 30, 1880, in Bangor, Me.; died Sept. 21, 1881, in Bangor.

(**221.**) Samuel Fullerton[7] Piper married Mary Jane Bragdon.

THEIR CHILDREN :

**323.** i. CARRIE LIZZIE[8] PIPER (*Samuel Fullerton[7]*, *Elisha[6]*, *Elisha[5]*, *Elisha[4]*, *Samuel[3]*, *Samuel[2]*, *Nathaniel[1]*), born Sept 28, 1868,
in Parsonsfield, Me.; a teacher ; graduated at Parsonsfield Free
High School.

**324.** ii. HATTIE MAY[8] PIPER (*Samuel Fullerton[7]*, *Elisha[6]*, *Elisha[5]*, *Elisha[4]*, *Samuel[3]*, *Samuel[2]*, *Nathaniel[1]*), born April 17, 1872,
in Parsonsfield, Me.; a teacher ; graduated at Parsonsfield Free
High School.

(**225.**) John Wesley[7] Piper married Ellen Adelaide Manson.

THEIR CHILD :

**325.** i. AUGUSTUS BURBANK[8] PIPER (*John Wesley[7]*, *Elisha[6]*, *Elisha[5]*, *Elisha[4]*, *Samuel[3]*, *Samuel[2]*, *Nathaniel[1]*), born June 4, 1868,
in Parsonsfield, Me.; a clerk.  He resides in Boston, Mass.

(**227.**) Horace Lord[7] Piper married Tryphena Stuart Gove.

THEIR CHILD :

**326.** i. JOSEPHINE LORD[8] PIPER (*Horace Lord[7]*, *Horace[6]*, *Jonathan[5]*, *Elisha[4]*, *Samuel[3]*, *Samuel[2]*, *Nathaniel[1]*), born June 11, 1864,
in Biddeford, Me.; married John Hopkins Foster, Dec. 28, 1887,
son of Alexander Hamilton and Martha (Hopkins) Foster, born
Jan. 31, 1862, in Evansville, Ind.; graduated at Indiana University in 1882, and at the Law School of Columbian University in

1884, receiving the degree of LL.B. He was admitted to the bar
in Evansville, in 1886, where he is now engaged in the practice
of his profession.—SEE THEIR CHILD : No. 351.

(226.) Mary Josephine[7] Piper married Oren Hooper.

THEIR CHILDREN :

327. i. FREDERICK NOAH[8] HOOPER (Mary Josephine[7] Piper,
Horace[6], Jonathan[5], Elisha[4], Samuel[3], Samuel[2], Nathaniel[1]), born
Oct. 16, 1865, in Portland, Me.; a merchant; married Hattie
Carlton Walden, daughter of Merrill and Mary Amelia (Carlton)
Walden, Jan. 25, 1888, born March 31, 1868, in Portland, Me.
He resides in Portland.*

328. ii. MARY JOSEPHINE[8] HOOPER (Mary Josephine[7] Piper,
Horace[6], Jonathan[5], Elisha[4], Samuel[3], Samuel[2], Nathaniel[1]), born
Aug. 18, 1867, in Portland, Me.; died Oct. 31, 1867, in Portland,
aged two months and thirteen days.

329. iii. MOSES ALBERT[8] HOOPER (Mary Josephine[7] Piper, Horace[6], Jonathan[5], Elisha[4], Samuel[3], Samuel[2], Nathaniel[1]), born June
30, 1869, in Portland, Me.; died April 14, 1870, in Biddeford,
Me., aged nine months and fourteen days.

(229.) Sherman Emery[7] Piper married Minnie Charlotte
Black.

THEIR CHILDREN :

330. i. GEORGE IRVING[8] PIPER (Sherman Emery[7], Irving[6], Jonathan[5], Elisha[4], Samuel[3], Samuel[2], Nathaniel[1]), born Aug. 9, 1879,
in Parsonsfield, Me.

331. ii. FRANK SHERMAN[8] PIPER (Sherman Emery[7], Irving[6],
Jonathan[5], Elisha[4], Samuel[3], Samuel[2], Nathaniel[1]), born July 5,
1884, in Parsonsfield, Me.

## NINTH GENERATION.

(232.) Ida Wallingford[8] Piper married John Torsleff.

THEIR CHILD :

332. i. LORENZO FRANCIS[9] TORSLEFF (Ida Wallingford[8] Piper,
Lorenzo Dow[7], Benjamin[6], Benjamin[5], Elisha[4], Samuel[3], Samuel[2],
Nathaniel[1]), born Dec. 20, 1873, in West Mitchell, Iowa.

---

*They have one child, Chester Walden, born May 23, 1889, in Port-
land, Me.

(**233.**) Mary Wallingford[5] Piper married Robert Waddell.

THEIR CHILD :

**333.** i. LOREN BURTON[9] WADDELL. (*Mary Wallingford[5] Piper, Lorenzo Dow[7], Benjamin[6], Benjamin[5], Elisha[4], Samuel[3], Samuel[2], Nathaniel[1]*), born July 13, 1880, in West Mitchell, Iowa.

(**243.**) Warren Taylor[5] Piper married Elizabeth Marlatt.

THEIR CHILD :

**334.** i. CHARLES HENRY[9] PIPER (*Warren Taylor[8], Perry H.[7], Ezekiel[6], David[5], Elisha[4], Samuel[3], Samuel[2], Nathaniel[1]*), born Nov. 2, 1867, in Malden, Ill.; a farmer ; married Clara Belle Jay, Feb. 3, 1886, born Feb. 10, 1868, in Malden, Ill. He resides in Malden. They have no children.

(**244.**) Charlotte[8] Piper married Joseph Johnston.

THEIR CHILDREN :

**335.** i. WILBUR[9] JOHNSTON (*Charlotte[8] Piper, Perry H.[7], Ezekiel[6], David[5], Elisha[4], Samuel[3], Samuel[2], Nathaniel[1]*), born Sept. 3, 1872, in Princeton, Ill.

**336.** ii. BERTHA[9] JOHNSTON (*Charlotte[8] Piper, Perry H.[7], Ezekiel[6], David[5], Elisha[4], Samuel[3], Samuel[2], Nathaniel[1]*), born Nov. 25, 1873, in Princeton. Ill.

(**245.**) Morgan Hiram[8] Piper married Honora Litchfield.

THEIR CHILDREN :

**337.** i. HARRY CLYDE[9] PIPER (*Morgan Hiram[8], Perry H.[7], Ezekiel[6], David[5], Elisha[4], Samuel[3], Samuel[2], Nathaniel[1]*), born Aug. 7, 1878, in Princeton, Ill.

**338.** ii. VERNA BELLE[9] PIPER (*Morgan Hiram[8], Perry H.[7], Ezekiel[6], David[5], Elisha[4], Samuel[3], Samuel[2], Nathaniel[1]*), born March 3, 1880, in Princeton, Ill.

**339.** iii. ELMER ROY[9] PIPER (*Morgan Hiram[8], Perry H.[7], Ezekiel[6], David[5], Elisha[4], Samuel[3], Samuel[2], Nathaniel[1]*), born Jan. 21, 1883, in Vinton, Iowa.

**340.** iv. PEARL MAY[9] PIPER (*Morgan Hiram[8], Perry H.[7], Ezekiel[6], David[5], Elisha[4], Samuel[3], Samuel[2], Nathaniel[1]*), born Apr. 22, 1888, in Vinton, Iowa.

(**247.**) Mary Lavinia[8] Piper married George Monroe Minier.

THEIR CHILDREN :

**341.** i. THEODORE HEINTZ[9] MINIER (*Mary Lavinia[8] Piper, David[5], Ezekiel[6], David[5], Elisha[4], Samuel[3], Samuel[2], Nathaniel[1]*), born Jan. 15, 1878, in Milo, Ill.

**312.** ii. GEORGE WILLIAM[9] MINIER (*Mary Lavinia[8] Piper, David[7], Ezekiel[6], David[5], Elisha[4], Samuel[3], Samuel[2], Nathaniel[1]*), born Sept. 6, 1879, in Milo, Ill.

**313.** iii. CLARENCE BUTT[9] MINIER (*Mary Lavinia[8] Piper, David[7], Ezekiel[6], David[5], Elisha[4], Samuel[3], Samuel[2], Nathaniel[1]*), born March 14, 1881, in Milo, Ill.

**314.** iv. IRA EZEKIEL[9] MINIER (*Mary Lavinia[8] Piper, David[7], Ezekiel[6], David[5], Elisha[4], Samuel[3], Samuel[2], Nathaniel[1]*), born Dec. 4, 1882, in Milo, Ill.

(**248.**) Ezekiel[8] Piper married Mary Elizabeth Harris.

THEIR CHILDREN:

**315.** i. BERTRAND[9] PIPER (*Ezekiel[8], David[7], Ezekiel[6], David[5], Elisha[4], Samuel[3], Samuel[2], Nathaniel[1]*), born March 7, 1879, in Hollowayville, Ill.

**316.** ii. WILLIAM[9] PIPER (*Ezekiel[8], David[7], Ezekiel[6], David[5], Elisha[4], Samuel[3], Samuel[2], Nathaniel[1]*), born Aug. 30, 1880, in Hollowayville, Ill.

**317.** iii. ALVA MAY[9] PIPER (*Ezekiel[8], David[7], Ezekiel[6], David[5], Elisha[4], Samuel[3], Samuel[2], Nathaniel[1]*), born May 5, 1884, in Hollowayville, Ill.

**255.** Viola Ann[8] Piper married William Sidwell Mercer.

THEIR CHILDREN:

**318.** i. LEWIS HIRAM[9] MERCER (*Viola Ann[8] Piper, Hiram Harding[7], Ezekiel[6], David[5], Elisha[4], Samuel[3], Samuel[2], Nathaniel[1]*), born May 30, 1881, in Malden, Ill.

**319.** ii. FRANK LEVI[9] MERCER (*Viola Ann[8] Piper, Hiram Harding[7], Ezekiel[6], David[5], Elisha[4], Samuel[3], Samuel[2], Nathaniel[1]*), born Oct. 27, 1883, in Malden, Ill.

(**275.**) Florence Amanda[8] Piper married Thomas William Griffin.

THEIR CHILD:

**350.** i. HARRY OWEN[9] GRIFFIN (*Florence Amanda[8] Piper, William Wilkinson[7], Ezekiel[6], David[5], Elisha[4], Samuel[3], Samuel[2], Nathaniel[1]*), born Jan. 3, 1878, in Selby, Ill.

(**326.**) Josephine Lord[8] Piper married John Hopkins Foster.

THEIR CHILD:

**351.** i. JOSEPHINE[9] FOSTER (*Josephine Lord[8] Piper, Horace Lord[7], Horace[6], Jonathan[5], Elisha[4], Samuel[3], Samuel[2], Nathaniel[1]*), born Nov. 30, 1888, in Washington, D. C.

## COPY OF THE WILL OF NATHANIELL[1] PYPER.

(From the Ipswich Records in Essex Registry of Deeds, at Salem, Mass., Book IV, Leaf 52.)

In the name of God, Amen. I, Nathaniell Pyper*, of Ipswich, in America, being weake in body, but of good and perfect memory, blessed be God, doe dispose of that estate God hath lent me, as followeth. *Imprimis:* I give unto Sarah, my loveing wife, my house and house lott, barne and orchard, and all my lands at Hog Island, with all my marsh both there and elsewhere in Ipswich, and all my stock of cattle and sheepe, with all my household goods and debts, dureing her widdowhood, and untill my children come to the age of one and twenty yeares, or be martyed. And then my will is that my daughter Sarah shall have five pounds payd her by her mother soe soone as she can convenyently ; also I give my son Nathaniell ten pounds at the age of one and twenty yeares, or at his day of marriage ; also I give unto all my other children, Josiah, John, Thomas, Mary, Margarett, Samuell, and Jonathan, five pounds apeece, as they come to age, or marry away : also my will is that none of these legases shall be payd soe as to hinder my wife her comfortable subsistence while she lives ; and also my will is that if any of my children shall depart this life before they come to age, that then there portions shall be equally devyded amongst the rest of my children that shall survive ; also my will is that if my wife should marry againe that she shall have one halfe of my house and halfe of my home lott dureing her naturall life, and the use of halfe my household goods ; after her decease my will is that my son Nathaniell shall have all my house and home lott ; and all my land at Hog Island, with the marsh there and elsewhere, all these being prised and equally devided amongst all my children then liveing, every one of them alike, only my son Nathaniell to have dubble portion out of the same. I doe make Sarah, my loveing wife, sole executrix of this my last will and testament, dated the seaventh day of March, in the yeare of Grace sixteene hundred seaventy and five, 1675. In wittness whereof I have hereunto sett my hand and seale.

NATHANIELL PYPER.    {SEAL}

These being wittnesses :
  FRANCIS WAINWRIGHT,
  JAMES CHUTE, SENR.

---

*This name was formerly spelled Pyper : but, as in some other English names, the y has been changed to i ; as, Pyke, Pike ; Smyth, Smith ; Hylton, Hilton. He sometimes spelled it Piper, and his children always spelled it so, as found in documents where they signed their names.

This will was proved by the oaths of Mr. Francis Wainwright
and James Chute to be the last will and testament of Nathaniell
Pyper to the best of their knowledge, and they saw him signe and
scale the same, and publish it to be his will in court held at Ipswich
this 26 of Sept., 1676.

As attest : ROBERT LORD, clerk.

————0————

## COPY OF THE INVENTORY OF THE GOODS AND CHATTELS
## . OF NATHANIELL[1] PYPER.

(From the Ipswich Records in Essex Registry of Deeds at Salem, Mass.,
Book IV, Leaf 52.)

An inventory of the goods and chattells of Nathaniell Pyper, late
of Ipswich, deceased, the 7th day of Aprill, 1676.

|  | £. | s. | d. |
|---|---|---|---|
| *Imprimis:* The dwelling house, barne and homestead . | 120 | 00 | 0 |
| Land at Hog Island . . . . . . . | 50 | 00 | 0 |
| 3 acres of marsh & a halfe . . . . . . | 09 | 00 | 0 |
| 2 oxen 9 £, three cowes 9 £ . . . . . | 18 | 00 | 0 |
| 13 sheepe & lambes . . . . . . . | 04 | 10 | 0 |
| 1 calfe 10s., three swine 40s. . . . . . | 02 | 10 | 0 |
| 1 mare & old horse . . . . . . . | 02 | 00 | 0 |
| IN THE PARLER. |  |  |  |
| 1 fether bed and furniture . . . . . . | 06 | 10 | 0 |
| 1 trundle bed, coverlett and bolster . . . . | 02 | 10 | 0 |
| a cubbard and a chest . . . . · . | 02 | 00 | 0 |
| a small chest 3s., & a longtable . . . . | 01 | 13 | 0 |
| 3 chaires 6s., andirons 7s. . . . . . . | 00 | 13 | 0 |
| earthen ware 4s., 2 small silver cups 15s. . . | 00 | 19 | 0 |
| a cradle & things in it . . . . . . | 00 | 14 | 0 |
| things in the cubbard . . . . . . | 00 | 10 | 0 |
| a box and a tubb in the clossett . . . . | 00 | 01 | 6 |
| a cushan & other things . . . . . . | 00 | 04 | 0 |
| a gunn and a cutlass . . . . . . | 02 | 00 | 0 |
| an old sithe . . . . . . . . | 00 | 01 | 0 |
| his weareing clothes . . . . . . | 05 | 00 | 0 |
| a small spoone 4s., weareing linnen 3 £ . . | 03 | 04 | 0 |
| 18 paires of gloves . . . . . . . | 00 | 09 | 0 |
| IN THE HALL. |  |  |  |
| pewter 2 £ 10s., brass 3 £ . . . . | 05 | 10 | 0 |
| pots, tramalls, & pothookes . . . . . | 01 | 00 | 0 |
| a warming pan, morter, & a spit 13s. . . . | 00 | 13 | 0 |
| occumy* spoones . . . . . . . | 00 | 03 | 0 |

* The word *occumy*, which is variously written occamy, ochimy, ocke-
my, means a mixture of fused metals, forming a compound resembling
silver, perhaps a kind of German silver. The elements of the composition
are not given in the books. The different modes of spelling are corrup-
tions of the word *alchemy*.

|                                                                                      | £. | s. | d. |
|--------------------------------------------------------------------------------------|----|----|----|
| 2 tables 12s., five chaires 6s. . . . . .                                             | 00 | 18 | 0  |
| tubbs & woodden ware 30s. , . . . .                                                   | 01 | 10 | 0  |
| earthen ware 7s., 2 fryeing-pans 5s. . . .                                            | 00 | 12 | 0  |
| a bible and bookes 10s., three wheeles 10s. . .                                       | 01 | 00 | 0  |
| 3 paires of cards 10s., 3 howes & an axe 10s. . .                                     | 01 | 00 | 0  |
| 42 lb. of woollen yarne . . . . . .                                                   | 04 | 04 | 0  |
| 10 lb. of linnen yarne 20s., 5 lb. of cotten yarne 10s. .                             | 01 | 10 | 0  |
| 8 lb. of cotten-woole 8s., 4 sives, 2 brushes, a baskett 6s.                          | 00 | 14 | 0  |

IN THE HALL CHAMBER.

|                                                                                      | £. | s. | d. |
|--------------------------------------------------------------------------------------|----|----|----|
| 15 lb. of sheepe woole . . . . . .                                                    | 00 | 15 | 0  |
| a trundle bed and other things 2 £ 10s. . . .                                         | 02 | 10 | 0  |
| flax 6s., onyons 4s. . . . . . .                                                      | 00 | 10 | 0  |
| corne and cheese 5s., 3 bushells of pease 12s. . .                                    | 00 | 17 | 0  |

IN THE PARLER CHAMBER.

|                                                                                      | £. | s. | d. |
|--------------------------------------------------------------------------------------|----|----|----|
| a fether bed & beding . . . . . .                                                     | 05 | 00 | 0  |
| a chest 4s., apples 10s. . . . . . .                                                  | 00 | 14 | 0  |
| hay & corne in the barne . . . . .                                                    | 04 | 00 | 0  |
| a box iron & brand iron 5s., 5 baggs 5s. . . .                                        | 00 | 10 | 0  |

‡ £265 18 6

Prised by us, James Chute, Nathaniell Rust.

Debts in the booke due about 30 £.

Debts oweing out of the estate 45 £.

Sarah Pyper, executrix to the last will of her late Husband, Nathaniell Pyper, upon oath testified this to be a true inventory of he estate to the best of her knowledge, in court at Ipswich, the 26th of Sept., 1676.

As attest : ROBERT LORD, clerk.

————o————

### STRATHAM SOLDIERS.

" A true list* of the Ninth Foot Company in the First Regiment in New Hampshire, belonging to Stratham, taken the 12th day of October, 1767.

OFFICERS.—Andrew Wiggin, Esq., Captain ; William Pottle, Jr., Lieutenant ; Simon Wiggin, Ensign ; Ebenezer Barker†, Clerk,

SERGEANTS.—Nathaniel Wiggin, Benja. Barker, Isaac Foss, Nathan Barker.

DRUMMERS —William Burley, Thomas Foss.

CORPORALS.—Daniel Mason, Andrew French, Samuel Piper, Jr.

PRIVATES.—Samuel Neal, Joseph Wiggin, Ezra Barker, John Avery, Jr., Jeremiah Avery, Joshua Avery, Thomas Wiggin, 3d, Daniel French, Joseph Hill, Jonathan Jewett, John Hill, Andrew Wiggin, Jr., Andrew Wiggin 3d, Samuel Lane, Jr., John Crocket,

---

‡ The value of a pound, in 1676, was about three dollars and sixty-five cents in our present currency.

* See page 84.　　　　　　　　　　　　　† See page 84.

Joseph Merrill, Jr., Benjamin Piper, Sargent Whicher. Joshua
Lane, Benja. Thirston. Daniel Jewell, Bickford Kenison. Nicklas
Wiggin, Samuel Kenison, Nahum Lary. Elisha Piper, Samuel Pot-
tle, Jonathan Wiggin, Jr., Jonathan Crocket. John Ford, Levy
Wiggin, Nathan Goss, Josiah Piper, Jr., Joshua Allen, Jonathan
French. Matthias French, Stephen Boardman, Jr., Jesse Wiggin,
Issacher Wiggin, Wheeler Burley, Roby Maston, Morris Clark, Na-
thaniel Wiggin. Jr., Samuel Kenison, Jr., John Piper. Samuel Wig-
gin, Jacob Jewett. Josiah Allen, Jude Allen, Jude Allen, Jr.. Moses
Clark, Thomas French. William French. Jr., Jonathan Taylor,
Richard Wiggin, Jacob Wiggin, Joseph Dennet. Moses Wiggin,
Samuel Allen, Jr., Jonathan Piper, Jr., Samuel Wiggin, Jr., Abner
Allen, Joseph Goss, Tutton Wiggin, Jr., Jacob Foss, Jonathan Foss,
David Crocker, Mark Wiggin. Elisha French. Chase Wiggin, Paul
Jewett, James Jewett, Samuel Leavitt, Jr., Thomas Piper, Jr., James
Clark, Chase Taylor, Jr., Nathan Piper, John Foss, Jonathan Leav-
itt, Jr., Jonathan Allen, Joseph Pevey, Ebenr. Eassman."

---

*I have copied this Company Roll from the one sent me by Cyrus Snell
Barker, of Cornish, Me. It was written by Ebenezer Barker, Clerk of the
company, one hundred and twenty-two years ago. Such a document
may seem foreign to a work on genealogy, but I think it will be interesting to the descendants of Ebenezer Barker, who was the father of the
Barkers who first settled in Cornish, and to those of Elisha[4] Piper, of
Parsonsfield, whose first wife, Sarah Barker, was his daughter; and
three of the company, Avery, Merrill, and Pottle, probably married his
sisters. It may, perhaps, be of interest also to other families whose ancestors are enrolled on it. The names are all spelled as I found them on
the roll sent me, and as I suppose the soldiers wrote them when they
signed the original roll.

† Ebenezer Barker was a son of Noah Barker, of Stratham, N. H., who
died there Jan. 3, 1749. Noah had a family of eight CHILDREN : Ruth,
Ezra, Benjamin, Nathan, *Ebenezer*, Ephraim, John, and Noah. Ebenezer married a daughter of Simeon Rundlet, of Stratham. She died Sept.
14, 1791, in Stratham, where they resided, aged seventy years. His father
gave him a deed, the original now (1889) in the possession of Cyrus W.
Barker, of Cornish, Me., of a lot of land in Stratham, containing twenty-
four acres, with a dwelling-house, barn, and orchard on the same, the
deed being dated March 26, 1739. Three of Ebenezer's sons and two of
his daughters settled in Maine, and one son and two daughters in New
Hampshire, and died in those States. He lived and died in Stratham,
and four of his children besides those mentioned died there. Cyrus
Snell Barker, his grandson, says : "The first Ebenezer Barker did not
settle in Cornish ; he only visited there." See his children who settled in
Maine and New Hampshire, pages 16 and 17. Most of the fact here
given, some of which were taken from the records of Stratham, were
furnished me by Ezra Barker of that town, and the remainder by Cyrus
Snell Barker.

# APPENDIX.

## GENEALOGY OF ASA⁴ PIPER,

### OF WAKEFIELD, N. H.,

## AND HIS IMMEDIATE DESCENDANTS.

### FIRST GENERATION.

**1.** NATHANIEL¹ PIPER*, ancestor of Asa⁴ Piper, was born in England about 1630, and emigrated to this country from Dartmouth, in Devonshire, probably as early as 1653. He settled in Ipswich, Mass.; married Sarah ——; and died in 1676, in Ipswich. She probably died in Wenham, Mass.—SEE THEIR CHILDREN : Nos. **2, 3, 4, 5, 6, 7, 8, 9, 10, 11, 12.**

### SECOND GENERATION.

(**1.**) Nathaniel¹ Piper married Sarah ——.

### THEIR CHILDREN :

**2.** i. SARAH² PIPER (*Nathaniel¹*), born about 1656 in Ipswich, Mass.; was living in 1675, being under twenty-one years of age; died.

**3.** ii. NATHANIEL² PIPER (*Nathaniel¹*), born June 25, 1658, in Ipswich ; died probably about 1689, in Ipswich.

**4.** iii. MARY² PIPER (*Nathaniel¹*), born Nov. 5, 1660, in Ipswich ; died Feb. 18, 1661, in Ipswich.

**5.** iv. JOSIAH² PIPER (*Nathaniel¹*), born Dec. 18, 1661, in Ipswich ; was living in 1675 ; died.

**6.** v. JOHN² PIPER (*Nathaniel¹*), born in 1663, in Ipswich ; married Lydia ——; died probably in Wenham, Mass. She died probably in Wenham.

**7.** vi. MARY² PIPER (*Nathaniel¹*) born Dec. 15, 1664, in Ipswich ; was living in 1690 ; died.

**8.** vii. THOMAS² PIPER (*Nathaniel¹*), born Nov. 26, 1666, in Ipswich ; married Grace Hawley, of Wenham, Nov. 21, 1692 ; died

---

* For a fuller account of Nathaniel¹ Piper and his children, see pages 11, 12, 13.

(85)

perhaps in Stratham, N. H., and his wife in the same place. It is
not certainly known whether he removed to Stratham or not. Some
of his connections think he did. It is certain that his sons, Thomas[3] and Nathaniel[3], settled there.

**9.** viii. MARGARET[2] PIPER *(Nathaniel[1])*, born June 16, 1668, in
Ipswich; married Tristram Greenleaf, Nov. 12, 1689; died. He
died.

**10.** ix. SAMUEL[2] PIPER *(Nathaniel[1])*. born June 12, 1670, in Ipswich; married Abigail Church, April 23, 1694; died Oct. 31, 1747,
in Stratham, N. H. She died in Stratham.

**11.** x. JONATHAN[2] PIPER *(Nathaniel[1])*, born in Ipswich, probably in 1672; married, 1st, Sarah Leach, of Boxford, Mass., May
7, 1695, who died May 6, 1700, in Ipswich: 2d, Alice Darby, of
Beverly. Mass., published Sept. 21, 1700: certificate granted Oct.
9, 1700. He died May 11, 1752, in Concord, Mass., to which
place he removed from Ipswich in 1731. She died April 23, 1758,
in Concord.—SEE THEIR CHILDREN : Nos. **13. 14. 15. 16, 17,
18, 19. 20. 21.**

**12.** xi. WILLIAM[2] PIPER *(Nathaniel[1])*, born in Ipswich; died
June 18, 1674. in Ipswich.

### THIRD GENERATION.

    **(11.)** Jonathan[2] Piper married, 1st, Sarah Leach :
        2d, Alice Darby.

THEIR CHILDREN :

**13.** i. SAMUEL[3] PIPER *(Jonathan[2] Nathaniel[1])*, born in Ipswich,
Mass., probably in 1700, a short time before the death of his mother Sarah ; died March 7, 1718, in Wenham, Mass.

**14.** ii. JONATHAN[3] PIPER *(Jonathan[2], Nathaniel[1])*. born in Ipswich, probably about 1702 ; married Abigail Bachelder, of Ipswich.
June 10, 1724, daughter of Joseph and Sarah Bachelder, born June
15, 1703. He removed to Concord, Mass., with his father in 1731.
Both were living Oct. 9, 1772. They probably died in Concord.

**15.** iii. NATHANIEL[3] PIPER *(Jonathan[2], Nathaniel[1])*, born in Ipswich; baptized March 17, 1706, in Wenham*; married Susanna
———, and settled in Concord. He died Aug. 2. 1758. in Concord.
She died after his decease, probably in Concord.

---

   * His father lived in Ipswich till 1731, but attended church in Wenham,
because it was nearer than the church in Ipswich ; therefore his children
were baptized in Wenham.

**16.** iv. JOSIAH³ PIPER (*Jonathan²*, *Nathaniel¹*), born in Ipswich; baptized Oct. 17, 1708, in Wenham ; married Sarah ——. After his marriage he lived a short time in Concord, and then settled in Acton, Mass. Both probably died in Acton.—SEE THEIR CHILDREN : Nos. **22. 23. 24. 25, 26. 27. 28.**

**17.** v. JOHN³ PIPER (*Jonathan²*. *Nathaniel¹*), born in Ipswich ; married Ruth ——, of Concord, before Jan. 22. 1747. They were living in Bolton, Mass., April 26, 1758, and probably died there.

**18.** vi. ALICE³ PIPER (*Jonathan²*, *Nathaniel¹*), born in Ipswich ; married Archelaus Adams, of Newbury, Mass., in 1726 ; died before Feb. 15, 1749. He died.

**19.** vii. SARAH³ PIPER (*Jonathan²*, *Nathaniel¹*), born in Ipswich ; married David Pierce. of Lexington, Mass.. May 9, 1734. Both were living April 26, 1758, in Harvard, Mass. They died.

**20.** viii. MARY³ PIPER (*Jonathan²*. *Nathaniel¹*). born in Ipswich ; married Joseph Gould. of Nottingham West (now Hudson). N. H., June 19, 1746 ; died. He died.

**21.** ix. JOSEPH³ PIPER (*Jonathan²*, *Nathaniel¹*), born in Ipswich, in 1718 ; married Esther Wright. daughter of Henry Wright, of Westford, Mass., Nov. 18. 1743 ; died Dec. 19, 1802, in Acton, Mass., to which place he removed from Concord in 1762, aged 85 years. She died April 7, 1808, in the same place, aged 85 years.

### FOURTH GENERATION.

(**16.**) Josiah³ Piper married Sarah ——.

THEIR CHILDREN :

**22.** i. SARAH⁴ PIPER (*Josiah³*, *Jonathan²*, *Nathaniel¹*), born Aug. 15, 1736. in Concord, Mass.; died.

**23.** ii. MARY⁴ PIPER (*Josiah³*. *Jonathan²*, *Nathaniel¹*), born July 26, 1739, in Acton, Mass.: died.

**24.** iii. JOSIAH⁴ PIPER (*Josiah³*, *Jonathan²*, *Nathaniel¹*), born March 2, 1743. in Acton ; married Sarah —— ; died. She died. They resided in Stow. Mass.

**25.** iv. ABIGAIL⁴ PIPER (*Josiah³*, *Jonathan²*. *Nathaniel¹*), born Feb. 14. 1746, in Acton ; died Oct. 31, 1753, in Acton.

**26.** v. SAMUEL⁴ PIPER (*Josiah³*, *Jonathan²*, *Nathaniel¹*), born Aug. 8, 1749. in Acton ; married Olive Adams, of Acton, June 29, 1772 ; died. She died.

**27.** vi. ELIZABETH⁴ PIPER (*Josiah³*, *Jonathan²*, *Nathaniel¹*), born May 8, 1752, in Acton ; died.

**28.** vii. ASA⁴ PIPER (*Josiah³, Jonathan², Nathaniel¹*), born March 7, 1757,* in Acton; a Congregational clergyman; married, 1st, Mary Cutts, born in Portsmouth, N. H., in 1766; died Jan. 4, 1802, in Wakefield, N. H.; 2d, Sarah Little, born in Kennebunk, Me., in 1765; died Oct. 15, 1827, in Wakefield. He graduated at Harvard College in 1778, studied divinity, and was ordained pastor of the Congregational Church in Wakefield, N. H., Sept. 22, 1785. He continued in that office for nearly fifty years, or until his death, having had a colleague only the last seven years of that time. He was a man of much force of character and deep piety. His judgment was sound, and his opinions on the great questions of his day, correct. He was much beloved by the members of his church and society, and by his townsmen generally. Rev. Albert H. Thompson, in his Address on the "One Hundreth Anniversary of the Organization of First Church, and Ordination of the First Settled Town Minister of Wakefield, N. H.," says of him : "He was of staunch English stock, a good scholar, and a priest of the Most High God. He was the first pastor of this church, and stands at the head of the line in time and talent." He was about six feet in height and of fine physical development. He died May 17, 1835, in Wakefield.—SEE THEIR CHILDREN : Nos. **29, 30, 31. 32.33.**

## FIFTH GENERATION.

(**28.**) Asa⁴ Piper married, 1st Mary Cutts; 2d, Sarah Little.

### THEIR CHILDREN :

**29.** i. ELIZABETH GERRISH⁵ PIPER (*Asa⁴, Josiah³, Jonathan², Nathaniel¹*), born Sept., 1789. in Wakefield, N. H.; married Porter K. Wiggin, Jan. 21, 1814; died in May, 1881, in Boston, Mass., where they resided. He died.

**30.** ii. EDWARD CUTTS⁵ PIPER (*Asa⁴, Josiah³, Jonathan², Nathaniel¹*), born Dec. 30, 1791, in Wakefield ; a farmer and deacon of the Congregational Church of Wakefield for nearly half a century. He entered Harvard College in Sept., 1809, one year in advance, and dissolved his connection with it at the end of his junior year, on account of ill health, which obliged him to abandon his intention of pursuing a professional life of study, and to adopt a busi-

---

*The time of his birth, as given by himself when he entered Harvard College, is March 17, 1757. The date March 7, given above, which is taken from the town records of Acton, Mass., is probably Old Style, and he added ten days for New Style, making it March 17, 1757.

ness which required labor in the open air. Rev. Albert H. Thompson in his Anniversary Address, makes the following quotation in regard to him : "He was the good old deacon, permitted for more than half a century to embellish, in his ancestral home, a hard-working farmer's life with the culture of a Christian gentleman. He had an apostolic beauty of character, and led a blameless life." He married Sarah Swasey (maiden name Sarah Jones), May 18, 1828, born March 18, 1790, in Portsmouth, N. H.; died Jan. 13, 1866, in Wakefield. He died Feb. 27, 1881, at his home in Wakefield. —SEE THEIR CHILDREN : Nos. **31, 35, 36.**

**31.** iii. ASA LEONARD⁵ PIPER *(Asa⁴, Josiah³, Jonathan², Nathaniel¹)*, born in 1798, in Wakefield ; a farmer ; died Nov. 2, 1844, in Wakefield, where he resided.

**32.** iv. MARIANNE⁵ PIPER *(Asa⁴, Josiah³, Jonathan², Nathaniel¹)*, born in 1801, in Wakefield ; married 1st, Jonathan Pollard, Sept., 1821 ; died ; 2d, Peter Horne, Jan. 18, 1824 ; died. She died in 1885, in Malden, Mass., where she resided.

**33.** v. SARAH LITTLE⁵ PIPER *(Asa⁴, Josiah³, Jonathan², Nathaniel¹)*, born in 1803, in Wakefield ; married Lewis Dearborn, Nov. 17, 1823 : died Nov. 19, 1831, at Great Falls, N. H., where they resided. He died.

## SIXTH GENERATION.

**(30.)** Edward Cutts⁵ Piper married Sarah Swasey.

### THEIR CHILDREN :

**34.** i. ADELINE⁶ PIPER *(Edward Cutts⁵, Asa⁴, Josiah³, Jonathan², Nathaniel¹)*, born April 8, 1829, in Wakefield, N. H.; died Dec. 15, 1831, in Wakefield.

**35.** ii. EDWARD CUTTS⁶ PIPER *(Edward Cutts⁵, Asa⁴, Josiah³, Jonathan², Nathaniel¹)*, born July 23, 1830, in Wakefield ; a machinist ; married Henrietta Cox, Aug. 16, 1852, born in 1830, in Searsmont, Me.; died Aug. 19, 1865. He died Nov. 22, 1862, in Wakefield. He resided in Boston, Mass.

**36.** iii. GEORGE FRANCIS⁶ PIPER *(Edward Cutts⁵, Asa⁴, Josiah³, Jonathan², Nathaniel¹)*, born Sept. 6, 1833, in Wakefield ; a farmer; married Mary Jenness, June 13, 1866, born Sept. 21, 1842, in Wakefield. He has rendered me valuable assistance in collecting genealogies for this book. See page 9. He resides in Wakefield, on the homestead of his grandfather, Rev. Asa⁴ Piper, which is pleasantly located near Lovewell's Pond, a beautiful sheet

of water, made memorable· by Capt. John Lovewell and his brave
men, who killed ten hostile Indians there at one time, in 1725.—
SEE THEIR CHILDREN : NOS. 37, 38.

## SEVENTH GENERATION.

(36.) George Francis⁶ Piper married Mary Jenness.

THEIR CHILDREN :

37. i. ADA FRANCES⁷ PIPER *(George Francis⁶, Edward Cutts⁵,
Asa⁴, Josiah³, Jonathan², Nathaniel¹)*, born March 27, 1867, in
Wakefield, N. H.; a teacher. She resides in Wakefield.

38. ii. IDELLA MAY⁷ PIPER *(George Francis⁶, Edward Cutts⁵,
Asa⁴, Josiah³, Jonathan², Nathaniel¹)*. born May 24, 1870, in
Wakefield ; a teacher. She resides in Wakefield.

————o————

## GENEALOGICAL RECORD.

A genealogical record of the ancestors, and brothers and sisters of
Rev. Asa⁴ Piper, of Wakefield, N. H., written by himself in 1833,
two years before his death.

"The great-grandfather emigrated from England during the Revolution in the days of Charles the First.   Which side he espoused in the
controversy, whether for the King or the Commonwealth, is now unknown.*   He came from Dartmouth, in the south-west of England,
and settled in Ipswich, Mass.   *  *  *   He had three or four sons.
My grandfather, I believe, bore the name of Jonathan ; he removed
to Concord.   His brothers' names were Nathaniel, Samuel, and
Thomas, if I am not mistaken.   Two of these went to Stratham ;
the other, I believe, died young.   I think there was one daughter,
if not more.   She married a Greenlief.   My grandfather had the
following children : Jonathan, Nathaniel, John, Josiah, and Joseph ;
and two daughters, one of whom married a Pierce ; the other a
Gould.   Josiah, my father, settled early in Acton, Mass., and left
three sons and three daughters; another daughter died at an early
age.   Joseph also settled in Acton, and had a large family.   These
spread in various directions, mostly in New Hampshire.   My oldest brother was named Josiah, the other Samuel ; my oldest sister
Sarah, the next Mary, the youngest Elizabeth, all older than my-
self."†

_____ ___ _____ ___ __ __ _____ __ ___

* He undoubtedly espoused the side of the Commonwealth.   All his
descendants in this country, of whom I have had any knowledge, have
been strongly in favor of a Republic, and have had no sympathy with a
Monarchy.   He was probably one of those who, foreseeing the restora-
tion of Charles the Second, emigrated to this country to enjoy greater
liberty than could be had in England.

† The genealogy of all his father's family is given on pages 87 and 88,
copied from the records of Acton, Mass.

# GENEALOGY OF SOLOMON¹ PIPER,

OF BOSTON, MASS.,

## AND HIS IMMEDIATE DESCENDANTS.

### FIRST GENERATION.

**1.** NATHANIEL¹ PIPER*, ancestor of Solomon³ Piper, was born in England about 1630, and emigrated to this country from Dartmouth, in Devonshire, probably as early as 1653. He settled in Ipswich, Mass.; married Sarah ——; and died in 1676, in Ipswich. She probably died in Wenham, Mass.—SEE THEIR CHILDREN : Nos. **2, 3, 4, 5, 6, 7, 8, 9, 10, 11, 12.**

### SECOND GENERATION.

(**1.**) Nathaniel¹ Piper married Sarah ——.

#### THEIR CHILDREN :

**2.** i. SARAH² PIPER (*Nathaniel¹*), born about 1656 in Ipswich, Mass.; was living in 1675, being under twenty-one years of age; died.

**3.** ii. NATHANIEL² PIPER (*Nathaniel¹*), born June 25, 1658, in Ipswich ; died probably about 1689, in Ipswich.

**4.** iii. MARY² PIPER (*Nathaniel¹*), born Nov. 5, 1660, in Ipswich ; died Feb. 18, 1661, in Ipswich.

**5.** iv. JOSIAH² PIPER (*Nathaniel¹*), born Dec. 18, 1661, in Ipswich ; was living in 1675 ; died.

**6.** v. JOHN² PIPER (*Nathaniel¹*), born in 1663. in Ipswich ; married Lydia ——; died probably in Wenham, Mass. She died probably in Wenham.

**7.** vi. MARY² PIPER (*Nathaniel¹*) born Dec. 15, 1664, in Ipswich ; was living in 1690 ; died.

**8.** vii. THOMAS² PIPER (*Nathaniel¹*), born Nov. 26, 1666, in Ipswich ; married Grace Hawley, of Wenham, Nov. 21, 1692 ; died

* For a fuller account of Nathaniel¹ Piper and his children, see pages 11, 12, 13.

(91)

perhaps in Stratham. N. H., and his wife in the same place.   It is
not certainly known whether he removed to Stratham or not.   Some
of his connections think he did.   It is certain that his sons, Thomas³ and Nathaniel³, settled there.

**9.** viii.  MARGARET² PIPER (*Nathaniel¹*), born June 16, 1668, in
Ipswich ; married Tristram Greenleaf, Nov. 12, 1689 ; died.   He
died.

**10.** ix.  SAMUEL² PIPER (*Nathaniel¹*), born June 12, 1670, in Ipswich ; married Abigail Church, April 23, 1694 ; died Oct. 31, 1747,
in Stratham, N. H.   She died in Stratham.

**11.** x.  JONATHAN² PIPER (*Nathaniel¹*), born in Ipswich, probably in 1672 ; married, 1st, Sarah Leach, of Boxford, Mass., May
7, 1695, who died May 6, 1700, in Ipswich ; 2d, Alice Darby, of
Beverly, Mass., published Sept. 21, 1700 ; certificate granted Oct.
9, 1700.   He died May 11, 1752, in Concord, Mass., to which
place he removed from Ipswich in 1731.   She died April 23, 1758,
in Concord.—SEE THEIR CHILDREN : Nos. **13, 14, 15, 16, 17,
18, 19, 20, 21.**

**12.** xi.  WILLIAM² PIPER (*Nathaniel¹*), born in Ipswich ; died
June 18, 1674, in Ipswich.

### THIRD GENERATION.

(**11.**) Jonathan² Piper married, 1st, Sarah Leach ;
                           `           2d, Alice Darby.

THEIR CHILDREN :

**13.** i.  SAMUEL³ PIPER (*Jonathan² Nathaniel¹*), born in Ipswich,
Mass., probably in 1700, a short time before the death of his mother Sarah ; died March 7, 1718, in Wenham, Mass.

**14.** ii.  JONATHAN³ PIPER (*Jonathan², Nathaniel¹*), born in Ips-
wich, probably about 1702 ; married Abigail Bachelder, of Ipswich,
June 10, 1724, daughter of Joseph and Sarah Bachelder, born June
15, 1703.   He removed to Concord, Mass., with his father in 1731.
He and his wife were living Oct. 9, 1772.   They probably died in
Concord.

**15.** iii.  NATHANIEL³ PIPER (*Jonathan², Nathaniel¹*), born in Ipswich, baptized March 17, 1706, in Wenham*; married Susanna
.——, and settled in Concord.   He died Aug. 2, 1758, in Concord.
She died after his decease, probably in Concord.

---

* His father lived in Ipswich till 1731, but attended church in Wenham,
because it was nearer than the church in Ipswich ; therefore his children
were baptized in Wenham.

**16.** iv. JOSIAH³ PIPER (*Jonathan²*, *Nathaniel¹*), born in Ipswich; baptized Oct. 17, 1708, in Wenham; married Sarah ——. After his marriage he lived a short time in Concord, and then settled in Acton, Mass. Both probably died in Acton.

**17.** v. JOHN³ PIPER (*Jonathan²*, *Nathaniel¹*), born in Ipswich; married Ruth ——, of Concord, before Jan. 22, 1747. They were living in Bolton, Mass., April 26, 1758, and probably died there.

**18.** vi. ALICE³ PIPER (*Jonathan²*, *Nathaniel¹*), born in Ipswich; married Archelaus Adams, of Newbury, Mass., in 1726; died before Feb. 15, 1749. He died.

**19.** vii. SARAH³ PIPER (*Jonathan²*, *Nathaniel¹*), born in Ipswich; ........ P... ... Piper, of Lexington Mass., May 9, 1734. Both were living April 26, 1758, in Harvard, Mass. They died.

**20.** viii. MARY³ PIPER (*Jonathan²*, *Nathaniel¹*), born in Ipswich; married Joseph Gould, of Nottingham West (now Hudson), N. H., June 19, 1746; died. He died.

**21** ix. JOSEPH³ PIPER (*Jonathan²*, *Nathaniel¹*), born in 1718 in Ipswich; married Esther Wright, daughter of Henry Wright, of Westford, Mass., Nov. 18, 1743; died in Acton, Mass., Dec. 19, 1802, to which place he removed from Concord in 1762, aged 85 years. She died April 7, 1808, in the same place, aged 85 years. SEE THEIR CHILDREN : Nos. **22, 23, 24, 25, 26, 27, 28, 29, 30, 31, 32, 33.**

### FOURTH GENERATION.

(**21.**) Joseph³ Piper married Esther Wright.

THEIR CHILDREN :

**22.** i. JOSEPH⁴ PIPER (*Joseph³*, *Jonathan²*, *Nathaniel¹*), born Nov. 18, 1744, in Concord, Mass.; married Elizabeth Hayward, of Acton, Mass. Both were living in Sharon, N. H., Feb. 14, 1807. They died.

**23.** ii. PHILIP⁴ PIPER (*Joseph³*, *Jonathan²*, *Nathaniel¹*), born July 6, 1746, in Concord; married Ann Gill, of Acton, Aug. 7, 1770; died Oct., 1776, in Acton. She died.

**24.** iii. ESTHER⁴ PIPER (*Joseph³*, *Jonathan²*, *Nathaniel¹*), born Feb. 20, 1748, in Concord; married, in Hollis, N. H., Jonas Brooks, of Acton, Aug. 31, 1774; died in Acton. He died.

**25.** iv. SIBYL⁴ PIPER (*Joseph³*, *Jonathan²*, *Nathaniel¹*), born Feb. 20, 1750, in Concord; married Francis Cragin, March 30, 1773; died May 16, 1809, in New Ipswich, N, H. He died Aug. 28, 1826, in New Ipswich.

**26.** v. JONATHAN⁴ PIPER (*Joseph³, Jonathan², Nathaniel¹*), born May 27. 1752, in Concord : married, 1st, Elizabeth Gibson, of Stow, Mass., Jan. 15, 1778 ; died in 1797 ; 2d, Martha ——, who survived him. He died July, 1807, in Ashby, Mass. She died.

**27.** vi. SOLOMON⁴ PIPER (*Joseph³, Jonathan², Nathaniel¹*), born Oct. 20, 1754, in Concord ; a farmer ; married Susanna Pratt, daughter of Rufus Pratt, Sept. 28, 1788, born Nov. 3, 1768, in Greenwich, Mass.   He was a man of great integrity ; served in the War of the Revolution ; was one of the party that went from Acton, where he then lived, to meet the British at Concord Bridge ; marched to Saratoga, N. Y., and was present at the surrender of Burgoyne at that place.   He was also with General Sullivan in Rhode Island.   "In politics he was a true Whig of the Federal stamp."   In person he was a little above the medium height, of active temperament, with light complexion and blue eyes.   In 1785, soon after the close of the war, he settled in Temple, N. H., but subsequently, in 1794, removed to Dublin, N. H., where he died Dec. 20, 1827.   She died June 27, 1844.—SEE THEIR CHIL-DREN : Nos. **34, 35, 36, 37, 38, 39, 40, 41, 42, 43, 44, 45.**

**28.** vii. RACHEL⁴ PIPER (*Joseph³, Jonathan², Nathaniel¹*), born Dec. 3, 1756, in Concord ; married, 1st, John Barker, in 1774 : died ; 2d, Daniel Barker, in 1792 ; died.   She died Apr. 14, 1838, in Waterford, Me.

**29.** viii. ALICE⁴ PIPER (*Joseph³, Jonathan², Nathaniel¹*), born Feb. 13, 1759, in Concord ; married Reuben Law, of Sharon, N. H., in 1778.   Both were living in Sharon Feb. 14, 1807.   They died.

**30.** ix. MARY⁴ PIPER (*Joseph³, Jonathan², Nathaniel¹*), born Dec. 18, 1763, in Concord ; married Amasa Piper*, July 23, 1782. He died Dec. 13, 1828, in Hancock, Vt.   She died July 27, 1839, in Hancock.

**31.** x. THOMAS⁴ PIPER (*Joseph³, Jonathan², Nathaniel¹*), born June 12, 1765, in Acton : married, 1st, Judith Powers, of Acton, May 11, 1788 ; died ; 2d, Sarah Ward, of Ashburnham, Mass., before 1808 ; died.   They resided in Weston, Vt., where their youngest child was born June 9, 1813.   He died.

---

* Amasa Piper is of the 5th generation.   His line of descent is as fol-lows : Amasa⁵, Jonathan⁴, Jonathan³ (brother of Joseph³), Jonathan², Nathaniel¹.

**32.** xi. Silas⁴ Piper (*Joseph³*, *Jonathan²*, *Nathaniel¹*), born April 25, 1767, in Acton ; married Mehitable Barker, of Acton, June 7, 1791 ; died in 1838, in Acton, on the homestead left him by his father. He was a man of great liberality and much force of character. She died in March, 1874, at the age of one hundred and three years. She was a remarkable woman, not only on account of her great age, but also for other qualities. Solomon³ Piper, in his book of genealogy, says of her : "Mehitable Barker descended from an ancient family in the town of Acton. Her comely form and benignant countenance, the faithful index of cheerfulness and contentment within, are the delight of all around her."

**33.** xii. Stuart⁴ Piper (*Joseph³*, *Jonathan²*, *Nathaniel¹*), born July 1, 1771, in Acton ; died July 10, 1771.

### FIFTH GENERATION.

(**27.**) Solomon⁴ Piper married Susanna Pratt.

### THEIR CHILDREN :

**34.** i. SOLOMON⁵ PIPER (*Solomon⁴*, *Joseph³*, *Jonathan²*, *Nathaniel¹*,) born July 19, 1789, in Temple, N. H.; married, 1st, Jerusha Hollis, Nov. 11, 1817, daughter of Daniel and Esther (Owen) Hollis, born April, 1780, in Boston, Mass., being older than her husband ; died Aug. 20, 1851, in Boston ; 2d, Mary Elizabeth Taggard, Nov. 4, 1852, daughter of William and Mary Trow (Welch) Taggard, born July 22, 1815, in Boston. She died April 19, 1888, in Cambridge, Mass. He was a merchant in Boston for more than fifty-five years ; a member of both branches of the City Council ; representative in the General Court ; and for twenty-three years President of the Freeman's Bank. He received a present of a service of plate from the Directors, "as a testimony of their confidence and respect." He was successful in business, and accumulated a large property. He died Oct. 15, 1866, in Boston. Portraits of him may be seen in the Histories of Temple and Dublin, N. H.—See their children : Nos. **46, 47, 48, 49.**

**35.** ii. Rufus⁵ Piper (*Solomon⁴*, *Joseph³*, *Jonathan²*, *Nathaniel¹*), born Feb. 14, 1791, in Temple ; a colonel ; married Anna Gowing, of Dublin, N. H., daughter of James Gowing, March 20, 1817. He died March 4, 1874, in Dublin. She died April 24, 1835, in Dublin. There is a portrait of him in the "History of Dublin, N. H.," and also one of his brother Cyrus.

**36.** iii. CYRUS⁵ PIPER (*Solomon⁴, Joseph³, Jonathan², Nathaniel¹*), born Dec. 30, 1792, in Temple ; married Catherine Greenwood, of Dublin, daughter of Joshua Greenwood, 2d, Feb. 2, 1815 ; died July, 1877, in Keene, N. H.   He died Jan. 29, 1877, in Keene.

**37.** iv. JONAS BROOKS⁵ PIPER (*Solomon⁴, Joseph³, Jonathan², Nathaniel¹*), born Dec. 4, 1794, in Dublin, N. H.; married Julia Greenwood, daughter of Moses Greenwood, of Dublin, Feb. 10, 1818 ; died Jan. 20, 1828, in Dublin.   She died May 4, 1884, in Dublin.

**38.** v. JOHN⁵ PIPER (*Solomon⁴, Joseph³. Jonathan², Nathaniel¹*), born Feb. 17, 1797, in Dublin ; married Prudence Greenwood, daughter of Joshua Greenwood, 1st, May 11, 1819, born in Dec., 1799.   He died Jan. 3. 1884, in Dublin.   She died Aug. 25, 1889, in Deerfield, Mass., aged 90 years, wanting about four months.

**39.** vi. SUSANNA⁵ PIPER (*Solomon⁴, Joseph³. Jonathan², Nathaniel¹*), born April 1, 1799, in Dublin ; died Jan. 5, 1800, in Dublin.

**40.** vii. SUSANNA⁵ PIPER (*Solomon⁴, Joseph³, Jonathan², Nathaniel¹*), born Dec. 28, 1800, in Dublin ; married Ira Gibbs, of Boston, Mass., Jan. 20, 1820.   She died March 7, 1821, in Boston.

**41.** viii. ARTEMAS⁵ PIPER (*Solomon⁴, Joseph³, Jonathan², Nathaniel¹*), born March 18, 1803, in Dublin ; married Maria Mason, of Dublin, daughter of Benjamin Mason. Sept. 21, 1824 ; died Jan. 24. 1828, in Dublin.   She died Jan. 26, 1880, in Marlborough, N. H.

**42.** ix. JAMES⁵ PIPER (*Solomon⁴, Joseph³, Jonathan², Nathaniel¹*), born April 1, 1805, in Dublin ; died Oct. 10, 1806, in Dublin.

**43.** x. EMILY⁵ PIPER (*Solomon⁴, Joseph³. Jonathan², Nathaniel¹*), born March 26, 1807, in Dublin ; married Ira Gibbs, of Boston, March 16, 1824, as his second wife.   She died Aug. 13, 1825, in Boston.   He died in Boston.

**44.** xi. HANNAH⁵ PIPER (*Solomon⁴, Joseph³, Jonathan², Nathaniel¹*), born Sept. 17, 1809, in Dublin ; married Jackson Greenwood, of Dublin, as his second wife, July 9. 1846.   He died Feb. 11, 1872, in Dublin.   She died Oct. 30, 1878, in Dublin.

**45.** xii. ELVIRA⁵ PIPER (*Solomon⁴, Joseph³, Jonathan², Nathaniel¹*), born Feb. 29, 1812, in Dublin ; married William Farnsworth, of Dublin, Nov. 26, 1829.   He died Nov. 14, 1851, in Dublin ; she died June 23, 1889, in Dublin.

## SIXTH GENERATION.

(**34.**) Solomon³ Piper married, 1st, Jerusha Hollis; 2d,
Mary Elizabeth Taggard.

### THEIR CHILDREN :

**46.** i. SUSAN ESTHER⁶ PIPER (*Solomon⁵, Solomon⁴, Joseph³, Jonathan², Nathaniel¹*), born Feb. 21, 1819, in Boston, Mass.; died
Aug. 18, 1820, in Boston.

**47.** ii. SARAH HOLLIS⁶ PIPER (*Solomon⁵, Solomon⁴, Joseph³, Jonathan², Nathaniel¹*), born Feb. 16, 1821, in Boston ; married Charles
Edwin Stratton, of Boston, Dec. 23, 1841. He died Dec. 4, 1872,
in Boston. She is now living in Boston.

**48.** iii. SUSAN ESTHER⁶ PIPER (*Solomon⁵, Solomon⁴, Joseph³ Jonathan², Nathaniel¹*), born July 22, 1823, in Boston ; married Bartholomew Welch Taggard, of Boston, Oct. 22, 1856. They now
live in Boston.

**49.** iv. WILLIAM TAGGARD⁶ PIPER (*Solomon⁵, Solomon⁴,
Joseph³, Jonathan², Nathaniel¹*), born Aug. 9, 1853, in Boston ;
graduated at Harvard College in 1874; Ph. D. of Harvard in
1883; married Anne Palfrey Bridge, July 10, 1879, daughter of
William Frederick and Elizabeth Guild (Crosby) Bridge, born in
Lexington, Mass., Dec. 19, 1854. He has rendered me valuable
assistance in collecting genealogies for this book. See page 8. He
resides in Cambridge, Mass.—SEE THEIR CHILDREN : Nos. 50, 51,
52.

## SEVENTH GENERATION.

(**49.**) William Taggard⁶ Piper married Anne Palfrey
Bridge.

### THEIR CHILDREN :

**50.** i. WILLIAM BRIDGE⁷ PIPER (*William Taggard⁶, Solomon⁵,
Solomon⁴, Joseph³, Jonathan², Nathaniel¹*), born Nov. 21, 1880, in
Cambridge, Mass.

**51.** ii. ELIZABETH BRIDGE⁷ PIPER (*William Taggard⁶, Solomon⁵,
Solomon⁴, Joseph³, Jonathan², Nathaniel¹*), born Sept. 19, 1883, in
Cambridge.

**52.** iii. ANNE TAGGARD⁷ PIPER (*William Taggard⁶, Solomon⁵,
Solomon⁴, Joseph³, Jonathan², Nathaniel¹*), born Sept. 26, 1887, in
Cambridge.

# GENEALOGY OF STEPHEN² PIPER,

## OF NEWFIELD, ME.,

## AND HIS IMMEDIATE DESCENDANTS.

### FIRST GENERATION.

**1.** NATHANIEL¹ PIPER\*, ancestor of Stephen⁵ Piper, was born in England about 1630, and emigrated to this country from Dartmouth, in Devonshire, probably as early as 1653. He settled in Ipswich, Mass.; married Sarah ——; and died in 1676, in Ipswich. She probably died in Wenham, Mass.—SEE THEIR CHILDREN : Nos. **2, 3, 4, 5, 6, 7, 8, 9, 10, 11, 12.**

### SECOND GENERATION.

(**1.**) Nathaniel¹ Piper married Sarah ——.

#### THEIR CHILDREN :

**2.** i. SARAH² PIPER (*Nathaniel¹*), born about 1656 in Ipswich, Mass.; was living in 1675, being under twenty-one years of age; died.

**3.** ii. NATHANIEL² PIPER (*Nathaniel¹*), born June 25, 1658, in Ipswich; died probably about 1689, in Ipswich.

**4.** iii. MARY² PIPER (*Nathaniel¹*), born Nov. 5, 1660, in Ipswich; died Feb. 18, 1661, in Ipswich.

**5.** iv. JOSIAH² PIPER (*Nathaniel¹*), born Dec. 18, 1661, in Ipswich; was living in 1675 ; died.

**6.** v. JOHN² PIPER (*Nathaniel¹*), born in 1663, in Ipswich ; married Lydia ——; died probably in Wenham, Mass. She died probably in Wenham.

**7.** vi. MARY² PIPER (*Nathaniel¹*) born Dec. 15, 1664, in Ipswich ; was living in 1690 ; died.

**8.** vii. THOMAS² PIPER (*Nathaniel¹*), born Nov. 26, 1666, in Ipswich ; married Grace Hawley, of Wenham, Nov. 21, 1692 ; died perhaps in Stratham, N. H., and his wife in the same place. It is

\* For a fuller account of Nathaniel¹ Piper and his children, see pages 11, 12, 13.

not certainly known whether he removed to Stratham or not. Some of his connections think he did. It is certain that his sons, Thomas⁴ and Nathaniel³, settled there.—SEE THEIR CHILDREN ; Nos. 12., 14, 15.

**9.** viii. MARGARET² PIPER (*Nathaniel¹*), born June 16, 1668, in Ipswich ; married Tristram Greenleaf, Nov. 12, 1689 ; died. He died.

**10.** ix. SAMUEL² PIPER (*Nathaniel¹*), born June 12, 1670, in Ipswich ; married Abigail Church, April 23, 1694 ; died Oct. 31, 1747, in Stratham, N. H. She died in Stratham.

**11.** x. JONATHAN² PIPER (*Nathaniel¹*), born in Ipswich, probably in 1672 ; married, 1st, Sarah Leach, of Boxford, Mass., May 7, 1695, who died May 6, 1700, in Ipswich ; 2d, Alice Darby, of Beverly, Mass., published Sept. 21, 1700 ; certificate granted Oct. 9, 1700. He died May 11, 1752, in Concord, Mass., to which place he removed from Ipswich in 1731. She died April 23, 1758, in Concord.

**12.** xi. WILLIAM² PIPER (*Nathaniel¹*), born in Ipswich ; died June 18, 1674, in Ipswich.

### THIRD GENERATION.

**(8.)** Thomas² Piper married Grace Hawley.

THEIR CHILDREN :

**13.** i. THOMAS³ PIPER (*Thomas², Nathaniel¹*), born Nov. 17, 1697, in Wenham, Mass.; removed to Stratham, N. H.; was selectman and auditor ; married Tabitha Rollins ; died Oct. 21, 1767, in Stratham, N. H., where he resided. She died in Stratham.— SEE THEIR CHILD* : No. 16.

**14.** ii. NATHANIEL³ PIPER (*Thomas², Nathaniel¹*), born Jan. 22, 1701, in Wenham ; removed to Stratham, N. H.; was surveyor of highways, constable, and selectman. He married and had children, but I do not know his wife's name nor the names of his children. He went to Stratham probably with his brother Thomas³,

---

*Since my manuscript was prepared for the press William T.⁴ Piper has ascertained from the Probate records of Rockingham County, N. H., now at Exeter, that Thomas³ Piper had several children, all of whom except the first are mentioned in his will, dated May 9. 1767, and proved Oct. 28, 1767. They are as follows : 1. Tabitha⁴, born June 5, 1729. 2. Stephen⁴, born May 14, 1733; married Abigail Church Wiggin. 3. Thomas⁴. 4. Jonathan⁴. 5. Patience⁴; married —— Wiggin. 6. Phebe⁴; married Joseph Page. 7. Abigail⁴; married —— Hill. 8. Henry Young⁴, born after 1746. They were all born in Stratham, N. H.

and died there Nov. 26, 1778.   A letter of administration of his estate was granted Jan. 12, 1779.

**15.** iii. PATIENCE³ PIPER (*Thomas²*, *Nathaniel¹*), born Feb. 25, 1703, in Ipswich ; died.

## FOURTH GENERATION.

(**13.**) Thomas³ Piper married Tabitha Rollins.

### THEIR CHILD :

**16.** i. STEPHEN⁴ PIPER (*Thomas³*, *Thomas²*, *Nathaniel¹*), father of Stephen⁵ Piper, of Newfield, Me., born May 14, 1733, in Stratham, N. H.; deacon of the Congregational Church of Stratham, and representative in the State Legislature.   He is said to be the ancestor of the Pipers in Sanbornton, N. H.   He married Abigail Church⁴ Wiggin, daughter of Captain Thomas and Sarah³ (Piper) Wiggin, June 20, 1754, born Aug. 28, 1737, in Stratham.   He died April 20, 1797, in Stratham, where he resided.   She died in Stratham.—SEE THEIR CHILDREN : Nos. **17, 18, 19, 20. 21, 22, 23, 24, 25, 26, 27, 28.**   •

### FIFTH GENERATION.

(**16.**) Stephen⁴ Piper married Abigail Church Wiggin.

#### THEIR CHILDREN :

**17.** i. MARY⁵ PIPER (*Stephen⁴*, *Thomas³*, *Thomas²*, *Nathaniel¹*), born Jan. 20, 1756, in Stratham, N. H.; married Andrew Jewett ; died.   He died.

**18.** ii. PATIENCE⁵ PIPER (*Stephen⁴*, *Thomas³*, *Thomas²*, *Nathaniel¹*), born Feb. 26, 1758, in Stratham ; married Noah Buzzell ; died.   He died.

**19.** iii. STEPHEN⁵ PIPER (*Stephen⁴*, *Thomas³*, *Thomas²*, *Nathaniel¹*), born June 23, 1760, in Stratham ; a farmer ; settled in Newfield, Me., in 1784 ; married, 1st, Mary Ayers, born Feb. 3, 1760, probably in Stratham ; died Aug. 15, 1800, in Newfield ; 2d, Widow Fogg, of Limerick, Me.; died in Newfield ; 3d, Widow Mary Martin, of Brookfield, N. H., born in Oct.. 1770 ; died Sept. 21, 1846, in Brookfield, aged 75 years and 11 months.   After the death of his second wife he removed to Brookfield, and died there April 26, 1826.*   The first seven children were by his first wife, the last

---

* This is the date given on his grave-stone in Brookfield, N. H., where he resided when he died ; that recorded in the town records of Newfield, Me., where he previously resided, is April 28, 1826.   I have no means of knowing which is the correct one.

two by the second, and·none by the third.—SEE THEIR CHILDREN : Nos. 29, 20, 21, 22, 23, 24, 25, 26, 27.

20. iv. ABIGAIL⁵ PIPER (Stephen⁴, Thomas³, Thomas², Nathaniel¹), born April 23, 1762, in Stratham ; married Simeon Cate ; died. He died.

21. v. NATHANIEL⁵ PIPER (Stephen⁴, Thomas³, Thomas², Nathaniel¹), born April 16, 1764, in Stratham ; resided in Sanbornton, and died there.

22. vi. SARAH⁵ PIPER (Stephen⁴, Thomas³, Thomas², Nathaniel¹), born April 8, 1766, in Stratham ; died in 1779, in Stratham, aged 13 years.

23. vii. ISRAEL⁵ PIPER (Stephen⁴, Thomas³, Thomas², Nathaniel¹), born July 4, 1768, in Stratham ; resided in Wolfborough, N. H.; died.

24. viii. ELIZABETH⁵ PIPER (Stephen⁴, Thomas³, Thomas², Nathaniel¹), born Nov. 5, 1770, in Stratham ; married Andrew Sanborn ; died. He died.

25. ix. TABITHA⁵ PIPER (Stephen⁴, Thomas³, Thomas², Nathaniel¹), born April 24, 1773, in Stratham ; married —— Chase ; died. He died.

26. x. THOMAS⁵ PIPER* (Stephen⁴, Thomas³, Thomas², Nathaniel¹), born Nov. 25, 1776, in Stratham ; kept the old farm in Stratham ; died.

* Rev. George Fisk Piper is a grandson of Thomas⁵ Piper, being of the 7th generation. His line of descent is as follows : George Fisk⁷, Thomas⁶, Thomas⁵, Stephen⁴, Thomas³, Thomas², Nathaniel¹. He was born March 23, 1837, in Boston, Mass.; graduated at Harvard Divinity School in 1862; first settled as a Unitarian minister in Houlton, Me.; then in Canton, Mass.; and now resides in Bedford, Mass., being pastor of the Unitarian Church of that town. He married Fannie Almira Duncan, June 10, 1863, born March 5, 1841, in Kittery, Me. They have five CHILDREN : 1. Carrie Emily⁸, born April 22, 1864, in Kittery ; married Stillman G. Whittaker, July 4, 1889. 2. Henry Duncan⁸, born Jan. 10, 1869, in Canton, Mass. 3. Fannie Maria⁸, born Sept. 24, 1870, in Canton. 4. Mary Alice⁸, born Nov. 6, 1872, in Canton. 5. George Fisk⁸, born Aug. 28, 1877, in Cambridge, Mass. They all reside in Bedford.

His father, Thomas⁶ Piper, was born in Stratham, N. H., June 15, 1809 ; married Caroline Tolman, of Boston, Nov. 25, 1834 ; died Sept. 12, 1880, in Stratham. His wife is living in North Cambridge, Mass. They had six CHILDREN : 1. George Fisk⁷, born as given above. 2. Henry⁷, born March 2, 1838, in Charlestown, Mass.; died Nov. 20, 1840, in Charlestown. 3. Carrie Louise⁷, born Aug. 17, 1840, in Stratham ; resides in North Cambridge. 4. Annie Mary⁷, born Feb. 10, 1843, in Stratham ; resides in

**27.** xi. HEPHZIBAH[5] PIPER (*Stephen[4], Thomas[3], Thomas[2], Na-thaniel[1]*), born Jan. 13, 1779, in Stratham ; married John Wiggin ; died.  He died.

**28.** xii. SUSANNA[5] PIPER (*Stephen[4], Thomas[3], Thomas[2], Nathaniel[1]*), born June 20, 1782, in Stratham ; married —— Coleman ; died.  He died.

### SIXTH GENERATION.

**(19.)** Stephen[5] Piper married, 1st, Mary Ayers ; 2d, Widow Fogg ; 3d, Mary Martin.

THEIR CHILDREN :

**29.** i. ISAAC[6] PIPER (*Stephen[5], Stephen[4], Thomas[3], Thomas[2], Nathaniel[1]*), born May 16, 1784, in Stratham, N. H., being six months old when his father settled in Newfield, Me.; married Sophia Chellis, born July 8, 1796, in Newfield.  He died Nov. 16, 1860, in Newfield.  She died Dec. 9, 1881, in Newfield.—SEE THEIR CHILDREN : Nos. 38, 39, 40, 41, 42, 43, 44, 45, 46.

**30.** ii. NANCY[6] PIPER (*Stephen[5], Stephen[4], Thomas[3], Thomas[2], Nathaniel[1]*), born Nov. 6, 1786, in Newfield ; married Winthrop Hill, of Waterborough, Me.; died Aug. 20, 1834, in Newfield.  He died in Newfield, where he resided.

**31.** iii. STEPHEN[6] PIPER (*Stephen[5], Stephen[4], Thomas[3], Thomas[2], Nathaniel[1]*), born Nov. 23, 1788, in Newfield ; married Louisa Parsons, daughter of Ensign Stephen and Abigail (Moore) Parsons, born in Parsonsfield, Me.  He lived in Newfield several years after his marriage, but subsequently went to the South, and died in Georgia.  She died.

**32.** iv. ABIGAIL[6] PIPER (*Stephen[5], Stephen[4], Thomas[3], Thomas[2], Nathaniel[1]*), born April 18, 1790, in Newfield ; married Charles Whicher, of Newfield, Jan. 20, 1810 ; died Aug. 12, 1869, in Newfield.  He died March 14, 1855, in Newfield.

**33.** v. JAMES[6] PIPER (*Stephen[5], Stephen[4], Thomas[3], Thomas[2], Nathaniel[1]*), born Sept. 9, 1792, in Newfield ; a sea-captain ; married Alice Perkins, of Kennebunk, Me ; died at sea.  His residence was in Kennebunk, where his wife was living at the time of his death.  She died.

North Cambridge.  5. Harriet Emma[7], born April 17, 1845, in Stratham ; married Augustus M. Lang, Sept. 10, 1879 ; resides in South Framingham, Mass.  (THEIR CHILDREN : 1. Roland S.[8], born Jan. 7, 1874, in Merrimac, Mass.  2. Russell A.[8], born Dec. 29, 1879, in Merrimac.)  6. Maria Abby[7], born Jan. 12, 1850, in Stratham ; resides in North Cambridge.

**34.** vi. PELATIAH⁶ PIPER (*Stephen⁵*, *Stephen⁴*, *Thomas³*, *Thomas²*, *Nathaniel¹*), born Sept. 9, 1795, in Newfield; married Mary Stevens, of Waterborough, Me.; died Jan. 17, 1837, in Newfield. She died in Newfield.

**35.** vii. ISRAEL.⁶ PIPER (*Stephen⁵*, *Stephen⁴*, *Thomas³*, *Thomas²*, *Nathaniel¹*), born Feb. 12, 1798, in Newfield; married Sarah Hill, of Newfield; died in South Boston, Mass. His residence was at Great Falls, N. H. His wife died at Great Falls.

**36.** viii. NATHANIEL.⁶ PIPER (*Stephen⁵*, *Stephen⁴*, *Thomas³*, *Thomas²*, *Nathaniel¹*), born Aug. 7, 1802, in Newfield; married, 1st, Mehitable Varney, of Newfield; 2d, Ruth Durgin, of Newfield. He died in Newfield, and his wives in the same place.

**37.** ix. THOMAS⁶ PIPER (*Stephen⁵*, *Stephen⁴*, *Thomas³*, *Thomas²*, *Nathaniel¹*), born July 2, 1804, in Newfield; married Sabrina Dunnells, of Newfield, and died there Sept., 1834. She died Sept. 16, 1865, in Iowa.

## SEVENTH GENERATION.

(**29.**) Asa⁶ Piper married Sophia Chellis.

THEIR CHILDREN :

**38.** i. MAHALA⁷ PIPER (*Asa⁶*, *Stephen⁵*, *Stephen⁴*, *Thomas³*, *Thomas²*, *Nathaniel¹*), born April 10, 1815, in Newfield, Me.

**39.** ii. HORACE⁷ PIPER (*Asa⁶*, *Stephen⁵*, *Stephen⁴*, *Thomas³*, *Thomas²*, *Nathaniel¹*), born Feb. 8, 1817, in Newfield; a farmer; married Lydia Moulton Dunnells, of Newfield, Nov. 1, 1840. He experienced religion when twenty-two years of age, and at the time of the organization of the Freewill Baptist Church in Newfield, Jan. 25, 1852, became an active and worthy member. In 1858 he was elected clerk, and in 1875 deacon, and continued to fill both offices till the time of his death, which occurred Sept. 17, 1886, in Newfield.—SEE THEIR CHILDREN : Nos. 47, 48, 49, 50.

**40.** iii. MARK FERNALD⁷ PIPER (*Asa⁶*, *Stephen⁵*, *Stephen⁴*, *Thomas³*, *Thomas²*, *Nathaniel¹*), born Feb. 21, 1819, in Newfield; married Elizabeth Davis, of Newfield. He resides at Wolfborough Junction, N. H.

**41.** iv. DAVID CHELLIS⁷ PIPER (*Asa⁶*, *Stephen⁵*, *Stephen⁴*, *Thomas³*, *Thomas²*, *Nathaniel¹*), born Nov. 30, 1821, in Newfield; married Elizabeth Hayes, of Limerick, Me. He died Jan. 10, 1852, in Newfield.

**42.** v. WILLIAM GILPATRICK⁷ PIPER (*Asa⁶, Stephen⁵, Stephen⁴, Thomas³, Thomas², Nathaniel¹*), born April 18, 1823. in Newfield; married Mary Trowbridge, of Newton, Mass. He died Aug. 18, 1876, at Mount Vernon, Me.

**43.** vi. JOHN CALVIN⁷ PIPER (*Asa⁶, Stephen⁵, Stephen⁴, Thomas³, Thomas², Nathaniel¹*), born July 9, 1825, in Newfield; married Mary Ann Clark. He resides in Bath, Me.

**44.** vii. MARY AYERS⁷ PIPER (*Asa⁶, Stephen⁵, Stephen⁴, Thomas³, Thomas², Nathaniel¹*), born July 4. 1827. in Newfield; married John M. Clark, of Limerick, Me. He resides in Bath, Me.

**45.** viii. LAVINIA DUNNELLS⁷ PIPER (*Asa⁶, Stephen⁵, Stephen⁴, Thomas³, Thomas², Nathaniel¹*), born, as given in the town records, Oct. 16, 1829, in Newfield; died Dec. 27. 1834. in Newfield.

**46.** ix. NANCY LAVINIA⁷ PIPER (*Asa⁶, Stephen⁵, Stephen⁴, Thomas³, Thomas², Nathaniel¹*), born Feb. 1, 1836, in Newfield; married Henry T. Carleton. She died May 27, 1873, in Wakefield, Mass.

## EIGHTH GENERATION.

(**39.**) Horace⁷ Piper married Lydia Moulton Dunnells.

THEIR CHILDREN:

**47.** i. SABRINA DUNNELLS⁸ PIPER (*Horace⁷. Asa⁶, Stephen⁵. Stephen⁴, Thomas³, Thomas², Nathaniel¹*). born June 27, 1843. in Newfield, Me.; married Frank Chadbourne, of Biddeford, Me., in 1867. She died Oct. 23. 1875. in Newfield.

**48.** ii. LEWIS LEANDER⁸ PIPER (*Horace⁷. Asa⁶, Stephen⁵, Stephen⁴, Thomas³, Thomas², Nathaniel¹*), born June 8. 1846. in Newfield; a machinist and farmer; married Estella Pauline Derbyshire, of Waltham, Mass., Dec. 25, 1886. He has rendered me valuable assistance in collecting genealogies for this book. See page 9. He resides in Newfield, on the homestead of his father. He has no children.

**49.** iii. JAMES FRANKLIN⁸ PIPER (*Horace⁷, Asa⁶, Stephen⁵, Stephen⁴, Thomas³, Thomas², Nathaniel¹*), born March 2. 1850. in Newfield; died April 4. 1850. in Newfield.

**50.** iv. CHARLES FREMONT⁸ PIPER (*Horace⁷, Asa⁶, Stephen⁵, Stephen⁴, Thomas³, Thomas², Nathaniel¹*), born April 29. 1858. in Newfield; married Della Davis, of Newfield, Jan. 24, 1878. He died July 20. 1884. in Newfield.—SEE THEIR CHILDREN: Nos. **51. 52.**

## NINTH GENERATION.

(**50.**) Charles Fremont⁸ Piper married Della Davis.

**51.** i. LOUIS DAVIS⁹ PIPER (*Charles Fremont⁸*, *Horace⁷*, *Asa⁶*, *Stephen⁵*, *Stephen⁴*, *Thomas³*, *Thomas²*, *Nathaniel¹*), born April 20, 1880. in Newfield, Me.

**52.** ii. EDWIN HORACE⁹ PIPER (*Charles Fremont⁸*, *Horace⁷*, *Asa⁶*, *Stephen⁵*, *Stephen⁴*, *Thomas³*, *Thomas²*, *Nathaniel¹*), born Jan. 17, 1883, in Newfield.

# INDEX TO ELISHA⁴ PIPER

* Names of persons not immediately connected with those whose genealogies are given are not included in this Index to Elisha⁴ Piper.

† The town and State at the right of the name denote the residence, if
given in the book : if not given, the place where born or died ; in the case
of young children, the residence of their parents.

# INDEX TO ELISHA‘ PIPER

AND HIS

## DESCENDANTS HAVING OTHER NAMES THAN PIPER.

# INDEX TO ASA⁴, SOLOMON⁵, AND STEPHEN⁵ PIPER

* Names of persons not immediately connected with those whose genealogies are given are not included in this Index to Asa⁴, Solomon⁵,
and Stephen⁵ Piper.

† The letters (As.) in parenthesis, annexed to the name, denote that the
person belongs to the Genealogy of Asa⁴ Piper; (So.), of Solomon⁵ Piper;
and (St.), of Stephen⁵ Piter.

‡ The town and State at the right of the name denote the residence of
the person, if given in the book; if not given, the place where born.

# INDEX TO ASA¹, SOLOMON³, AND STEPHEN² PIPER

## AND THEIR IMMEDIATE

# DESCENDANTS HAVING OTHER NAMES THAN PIPER.

- - - - -